Spirits Fly High

The Continuing Narrative of a Mediums Journey
(Part Three of a Trilogy)

Lynn Quigley

First Published and Printed in the UK

Spirits Fly High

The Continuing Narrative of a Mediums Journey
(Part Three of a Trilogy)

Lynn Quigley

The purpose of this book is to inform and entertain - it contains the
personal views, memories and thoughts of the author – It is not a
training manual. The author and or Publisher shall have neither
liability nor responsibility to any person or entity with respect to
any loss or damage caused, or alleged to have been caused, directly
or indirectly, as a result of any person taking it upon themselves to
copy any activity or act on any information as described within it's
pages. Neither does the author and or publisher advocate seeking
alternative therapy in the place of medical assessment and opinion.

Published by
J & L Quigley
P.O Box 122
Penmaenmawr
LL30 9AJ
UK

First Edition, 2009
ISBN 978-0-9534946-5-1

Published and Printed in the UK

Dedication

This book is dedicated to my husband John.

John,

You always said, as I came to the end of writing "More friends than You Know", that you saw the story as a trilogy.

Well – here we are – "Spirits Fly High" – the finale.

So this book is for you.

Over the years, you have given me your support, enthusiasm, encouragement and vigilance.

Those things give me freedom to fly.

Together – we have produced the three books – and there is as much of your spirit in them - as there is mine.

Now that this work is done – my wish is that you will allow yourself the time to finish writing your own, much awaited books.

**** ******

Lynn

Epigraph

Cautiously, I stood up and began my descent down the pathway – carefully placing one foot in front of the other. At first I stumbled on the stones that made up the pathway – and I asked for help once more. Although there was no light whatsoever – I found that when I looked down onto the path – I instinctively knew where the bigger, more hazardous stones were and could therefore avoid them.

I soon realised that if I just walked with Trust and Confidence – I would not stumble

(extract from Chapter One)

With one movement – the passport was opened, stamped, and slid back towards me.

I even glimpsed a hint of a smile as he said the words: "Have a nice daaay."

Picking my passport up – I smiled and thanked him.

"Next" – he shouted

(extract from Chapter Two)

This short walk led me to what I feel - is the most wonderful spot on the whole planet.

A place where the clear sparkling river widens and rushes over rocks, creating eddies and pools that sparkle in the sunlight. And the backdrop to this brilliant place – and towering into the sky – is the most tremendous view of Cathedral Rock.

(extract from Chapter Three)

Contents

Acknowledgements

I wholeheartedly thank Joy and Sandra for their kindness and generosity.

Without their unexpected invitation to visit them and without their unique spiritual gifts –

I would not have been able to write this part of the story under the title of "Spirits Fly High."

Joy and Sandra gave my "Team" in Spirit and I, a wonderful opportunity - I am eternally grateful.

Joy and Sandra,
Thankyou for your friendship – and thankyou for all the wonderful memories.

Foreword

"Spirits Fly High" is the last part and concluding book in a trilogy.

As with the other books written by Lynn Quigley, it is a heartfelt recollection of her Spiritual Journey. "Spirits Fly High" is the culmination of the part of her journey at a particular time in her life in which Lynn honours the request made many years earlier by her Spirit guides to share the experience of finding and establishing a loving and timeless awareness and connection with those in Spirit

In her first book of the series "More Friends Than You Know", Lynn wrote about the development of her natural communication skills with the world of Spirit. The result was a down to earth, inspirational, moving and frequently humorous story.

In reading it, you learned of the method, which Spirit used in training her to work the way she does, getting the amazing communication she gets without any fuss, ritual or drama.

In her second book, Lynn continued to share the journey with you, by re-visiting experiences – happy, sad, painful and joyful - from many years of personal memories, bringing to you more of the techniques and communication given by Spirit, in another brilliant and extremely well received book "Spirits In The Sky."

And now – for those of you who have read the first two parts of this trilogy – she brings you the conclusion. Part three "Spirits Fly High" is another seamless continuation of the much awaited story which took Lynn to America – her first experience (in the physical world) of flying, visiting another country and the "Highs and Lows" of that trip along with the ensuing emotions and feelings associated with the arrival and departure of her Spirit Guides.

For those of you who have not read the previous two books, "Spirits Fly High" can be read as a "stand alone" volume bringing laughter, joy and wonderment tinged with some sadness but always with the love and wisdom that direct communication with Spirit brings.

I've said this before and I make no excuse for saying it again.

Every day that goes by, Lynn's insight, guidance, love and understanding help me, and many others move forward through this life and I consider it a great privilege as well as a pleasure that we travel this path together.

Lynn's books are said by many to be "Life Changing" and although this final part of the trilogy is now complete and with it her "contract" with Spirit to write it – she has already embarked on a series of other publications about ...... well – that's another story – one which Lynn will tell you about, another time.

John Quigley

Preface

This part of my story begins at Christmas time 1997.

Since the late summer of 1994 – I have been working with my Spirit Guide – Silver Cloud.
On the 11th of November that year my previous doorkeeper - Buffalo - had left to become a guide to another channel and a new doorkeeper – Wolf - had entered my life.

The role of a doorkeeper is very important. He or she provides protection to both those in the physical and to those within the Spirit world – thus allowing communication to take place within a safe environment. Both Silver Cloud and Wolf are Native American Indians.

Silver Clouds' own Guide – White Cloud – was also a frequent visitor, as was Peter, a Spirit who has never been mortal and therefore could be described as "alien."

Silver Cloud, Buffalo, White Cloud and Wolf – are my "Spirits In The Sky."

Using their combined attributes of – clear instruction – sternness – humour – and unfailing care and love – they have taught me - "step by step" and safely - to communicate not only with them – but with other Guides and loved ones.
Introducing myself and others to a whole host of visiting Spirit.

Through this communication, we have been able to assist other channels – in particular – Healing Channels like my husband John – in their work with their patients and "Earth Energy" healing.

My Spirit team and John's team of Spirit Guides, plus, loved ones in Spirit – have walked with John and I through times of hardship and uncertainty, including bankruptcy and the subsequent loss of our home and business.

Their advice, support and guidance has been immeasurable and were it not for their help – I feel that I would have easily "lost my way" in life.

Silver Cloud, Buffalo – and now Wolf - have performed many Spirit releases through me. Not in a spectacular fashion – but in a calm, relaxed manner. I have witnessed many a happy reunion in the Spirit World as a consequence of the ministrations of them and others in the Spirit World, who have come to assist at the time. Every step I take – Silver Cloud, Buffalo and Wolf have been beside me.

Silver Cloud does not like standing in supermarket queues – and Wolf loves driving in the car!

Both of them think the bathroom is a good place to communicate with me – whatever I am doing in there!!

And both of them have tirelessly ignored my "tantrums" and impatience and given me their unconditional love.

I, in turn, have always tried to show the great love and respect that I have for each of them - although my temper gets the better of me sometimes. However – given that I am nowhere near "perfect" – our relationship is one of respect, gratitude and above all – love.

So – returning to the story.

The Bankruptcy is behind us, and John and I are living in a secluded, rented cottage called "Garth". The cottage is in Denbighshire, North Wales.

John has been on a residential course run by two American Ladies called Joy and Sandra.

During his stay – he asked me to speak with one of the ladies who had a problem. She hoped that my "Team" could give her some advice – which they did – and the problem was resolved.

This one telephone conversation began a "telephone" friendship, which continued over the next 4 or 5 months after their return home to Arizona in America.

MY WORK WITH SPIRIT.

I would like to use the following pages *(from "Spirits In The Sky")* to describe the type of work that I do.

All the work is confidential and any notes that I need to make at the time – are destroyed soon after.
So – the following anecdotes are all written from memory and will be somewhat sketchy, in detail.

Music.

Music has been a passion of mine since I was born.
My parents both sang in a choir and my weekly attendance at Methodist Church – from a toddler – up to 16yrs old – gave me a love of Organ music and singing. Two adult, childhood friends of mine - introduced me to Opera, the Trumpet and Trombone.
My red Dansette Radio, introduced me to "pop" music.

As a child I had piano lessons - but gave them up when I was about 11 – 12 yr. old.
I taught myself to strum a guitar – badly.
In my 20s and 30s, I owned a piano, electric organ, drum kit and a Kareoke machine.

Being master of none of these instruments – you can imagine the noise that I produced! Did I mention – I like to play music loudly!

I use music to reflect or alter my moods – and can spend hours, shut in a room, listening to a variety of tunes in order to achieve that.

My music collection is diverse and Spirit have used that diversity to communicate with me:

Communicate through the words of a song or –
through my listening to their chosen piece – helping me
to move forward – "travel" with them - resolve issues
and heal.

I feel so fortunate to have this avenue open to me.
Each Guide and doorkeeper that I have worked with
has used music, and that - combined with their
unconditional love – has truly, saved my sanity – on
more than one occasion.

My Guides sometimes guide me to play a piece of
music for someone who has come for a sitting or has
just come to visit, and, at their suggestion and with their
guidance, I have made compilation tapes to send to
people.

But – work aside – I have to say - I just love music!

From Abba to Andrea Bocelli.
And my personal favourites of the "New World Music"
genre are – David Sun. Stephen Rhodes. Asha.
Medwyn Goodall and Pia.

Distant Healing.

In 1994 I was watching the television, when a news
story came on. The report told of a child whose
mysterious illness, was baffling the medical team that
were looking after him.
They were at a loss as to what treatment they could try
next. There was film showing the child in his hospital
bed – he looked barely conscious

The boy's parents and family were devastated, as the
child was becoming weaker by the day.

Moved by the plight of the child, his family and the medical staff – I sat and wished that "something" could be done to help them.

I knew that Spirit were around watching and caring for me – so I decided to sit and ask them for help for the boy, and that is what I did – and - knowing that there would be many other people around the country - who had also seen this report – I knew that my voice would not be a "lone" voice.

Many months later – I happened to pick up a magazine in a Newsagent. Flicking through the pages – I saw a feature about the "miraculous" recovery of a child – who had been close to death.

The child that the article was referring to – was the child I had seen previously on the television
I began to read the reporters words: The doctors - it said - remained confounded by his illness – and - his subsequent recovery. Accompanying the article was a photograph of the child and his family. The photograph showed a group of happy smiling faces.

I was stunned by the boy's recovery.
I was thrilled to bits – to see their smiling faces, and I was very grateful to Spirit, for leading me to pick up that magazine which contained that article.

I continue to ask for distant healing – but unlike that first time – when I had no communication – I now receive communication.

Sometimes, I am told that my request has *"been noted"* and then I am dismissed. Sometimes, I stand and witness the healing being given by Spirit. Sometimes, I am involved myself:

I will act as a communicator to the patient – having been given facts about their illness. When communicating with the patient – I invariably find that they have a message to pass to someone, and "we" can advise them on the best way to deliver that message.

Always – I ask permission of my Guides and the patient (be that physically or spiritually) – before I proceed.
Always - I listen to - and respect and abide by - their answer, and – always – in the case of children – I ask permission from the parent or guardian - before I ask my Guides and the child itself.

The word distant – only relates to the fact that I am not with that person physically. Remotely my spirit travels to that person - and for me to go without permission – would be unforgivable, rude and egotistical.

That is my unwritten rule.

An uninvited and unwanted visitor – as we can all relate to – is often not welcome, and an uninvited and unwanted travelling spirit can be very distressing. These rules apply to people – animals and land.

If I am asked by a third party, to send some healing for a friend, relative or acquaintance – I cannot proceed until I have been given permission from my Guides and from the persons Higher Self.

My answer to them is always – "I will ask" on the understanding that if my request if denied – I cannot help.

Healing into death.

In 1991 – as my dad lay in a hospice a couple of miles from our house – from my vantage point in our living room - I saw the clouds in the sky – part, in the distance. The light that emitted through the clouds seemed to be descending onto the roof of the hospice.
Knowing that dad was now peaceful – and near to death, I "spoke" to him:
"Go to the Light – Go up into the Light dad."

In the early hours of the next morning – my dad died.

That was my first experience of healing into death.

From then on – and now working with my Guides – I have worked, remotely - with men, women, children and animals – who are close to death.
Unlike that first time - I am now given information and the opportunity to converse with the Spirit of the departing – and they with me.

I work with a combination of - my own Guides – the patient - Guides and loved ones in Spirit connected to the patient – Angels – and those loved ones who will be left behind to grieve.

As in the case of distant healing – sometimes I am directly involved and sometimes I am privileged to witness the workings of the Spirit World - as a bystander.

This work is usually done over a period of days – and Spirit guide me on that matter. but sometimes – the combined work of Spirit and the patient – is completed

very quickly. Often I will play music – the title of which is chosen by my Guides or the patient.
The music, lending its healing tones and/or words – to the patient.

I remember one elderly gentleman who was clinging to life. He asked for the song "I want to know where love is?" The words of the music were his way of expressing his fear – the fear that made him cling to life.

And his fear was - that once he died – there would be no one around to love him. Playing the message for him let him know that he was being listened to. Let him know that his Spirit could be heard. It allowed him to realise that he was not alone, and as that realisation grew – I witnessed his surprise at seeing Spirit around him, and I witnessed the relief that swept through him as he saw a familiar face approach.

His face lit-up like a beacon – as his mother walked towards him – her arms outstretched in greeting.

Assisting - healing into dying - is always a privilege.
It is always moving. There can be angst, upset or anger before peace is found - and occasionally, when the work is nearly completed - there can be one or two jokes along the way.

Always – there is the unconditional love shown by all those in Spirit who come to assist.
Always – there is a Guiding Light – whose Soul purpose is to assist in that walk between the physical life and everlasting life. Always – there is a celebration to honour the returning Soul.

Several years ago, a neighbour of ours died. I didn't know them that well, and had no plans to attend the funeral. However, the day before the funeral, I was asked by Spirit to go. When I asked why – I was told that two family members were holding their loved one to them – which meant that the Spirit of the person would be held to the Earth.

That Spirit was already in shock at their death – and needed to enter the Spirit World for some rest and recuperation. As I sat at the rear of the Church – I asked for the "appropriate" Guides and helpers to assist.
I could feel the presence of our neighbour as her family held her to them – and then I felt the descending presence of Spirit. The Spirit helpers gathered our neighbour into their energy and I watched, as they hovered over the family as they sat in the pews.

I was told that she was asking the two members of her family to let her go – whilst assuring them that she would return at sometime in the future.

A few seconds later, the combined Spirits left the confines of the Church, I was told – *"We have got her. Your work is over."*

I have never been asked to attend another funeral by Spirit – but I have been to several since then.
I always make a point of saying to Spirit – "If there's anything I can do – just ask."

There seems to be two distinct beliefs regarding the question "Does Spirit recognise our time" – as in Greenwich Mean Time.
Some people will tell you that "Time means nothing to the Spirit World" – and others will say that they

understand our GMT – and they work with us on that scale. In my experience – both beliefs are true.

In my experience – when Spirit say, *"soon"* or, *"later"* that can mean anything between, the next minute and the next few years, but - Silver Cloud taught me that if he said *"Come back in 10 minutes."* - He meant 10 minutes - not 11 minutes. *"9am sharp!"* meant 9am – not five past. So all I can say, is that Spirit uses GMT as a time zone - Sometimes!

That is why, that on the night Silver Cloud told me that Nipper, our Goldfish would die at 2am – I knew that this would be the case.

Nipper had lived with our two other fish, in a large aquarium. The other fish had bullied him – keeping him away from the food until they had their fill, but over the years – Nipper had survived his two rivals and a large cyst over one of his gills, and - having the aquarium to himself – had grown into a large sturdy Goldfish.

Nipper had been the first member of our family to move into Garth, as we had taken him over the day before we moved. Lately, he had been off his food for short periods – and now his dorsal fin was laid down on his back and his sense of balance was failing.

Neither John nor I could entertain the idea of killing him – so we let "nature take its course."
But nature was being very slow – and for two weeks, Nipper hovered between life and death.
Then came those words from Silver Cloud,
"He will die at 2am."
I sat up with the fish – tears of helplessness overwhelming me.

At 1.50am – he was still alive.
At 2am – he died.

Nipper had been our constant companion for 25years.
Throughout his life, we had kept the aquarium out of the sun – as it fouls the water – now - sunshine would no longer be a hazard to Nipper.
We buried him in the garden at Garth – choosing a lovely sunny spot in the grass.

As I said before – I can find myself working with Guides, patients, loved ones and Angels.
I have travelled to hospital rooms were the light of Spirit is so bright - it hurts your eyes.
I have witnessed Spirit doctors tending to patients.
I have witnessed Angels waiting in silent serenity – waiting to lead a patient home. I have witnessed patients happily chatting to their Spirit visitors – prior to them departing this life.

But – I was not prepared for the "healing into death" that took place when Johns' dad – also named John – was in the hospice. John had told this story himself and is happy for me to tell you now.

Early morning on the 6th March 1997 – as I have already mentioned – John was taken into a hospice.
John and his sister had both been to see him – and I had planned to go the next day – although I must admit - it was with some trepidation, having being told that he was in the same bedspace as my dad had been, some six years earlier.

My communication with Spirit – and healing into death experiences has not eradicated the memories that I have – seeing my dad in the hospice, both before and after he had died. But I knew that those memories would have to be left in the car park, when I went to visit John.

At 12.40 p.m. on the 6th March I was told that John was very restless. I "raised my vibrations" and asked for distant healing for John – and then I asked if there was anything I could do.

I was told to hold a particular quartz crystal that I had, and went off to get it. Holding the crystal in my hand - I went with Silver Cloud to stand at John's bedside.

There were many Spirits around his bed – all glowing and radiating light – so that from my position at the end of the bed – their energy was intertwined.

Out from the energy emerged one Spirit – I knew this was John's own father. A man who I referred to as John's "Scottish granddad."

Scottish granddad approached the bed and leant over John. "You are acting like a child!" he accused.

He then leant over John and thumped him hard in the chest – just once. Not – I knew – to start his heart – but to stop it.

I was horrified.

"We can make the decision for you – if you don't make it yourself." He continued – albeit in a softer voice.

I had never witnessed anything like this – I couldn't understand these words and the action.

I was shocked and looked to Silver Cloud to see his reaction. He just smiled.

And John went into a restful sleep.

I "returned to my chair" still in a state of shock.

That evening – John returned from visiting his dad and told me that his dad had become restless during the afternoon and had been sedated – adding, that whilst visiting him – John had suddenly thumped his own chest – just once. However – when John and his sister had left the hospice that evening, my father-in-law had been quite contented and happy and had settled down for his first night in the hospice.

Much later that night – Silver Cloud urged me to "travel" to John's bedside.

I raised my vibrations and with Silver Cloud by my side I arrived at John's bedside. The small ward was dimly lit and through that dim light – John and I began to walk towards a very bright light. This was a walk that we had taken before but this time I felt a very real sense of tension and apprehension.

We continued to walk side by side, down a very brightly lit tunnel, which had appeared in front of us. The tunnel expanded further into the distance as we walked, and the brightness was excruciating.
The further we walked – the brighter the light became.
Through the brightness and in the far distance, we both saw the hazy shadows of many standing figures. John hesitated momentarily and paused. I waited, knowing that John was deciding whether to continue this walk.

John took another pace forward and together we continued our slow walk towards the brightest of white light. Emerging out of the tunnel, and standing a few yards away from us, we could clearly see figures. The figures were standing in rows, unspeaking, yet smiling as in greeting. John gasped as he recognised his parents and brothers, behind them, more spirits were standing –

waiting. The bright white light created a milky haze that obscured everything – everything that is – except for those serene smiling faces.

Their energy was awesome.

Throughout my travels into the Spirit world I had seen other bright lights – I had walked towards white light – I had been surrounded in white light – but I knew that this experience was different – very, very special.

I went to step towards the waiting Spirits - Silver Cloud blocked my way.

"You cannot go any further" he commanded.

In an instant – I understood that I was at THE place of no return. I looked down onto the ground and saw, just two paces in front of me, a narrow line.

A line – invisible - yet visible.

A line - that only those who have forsaken their physical bodies can cross. A line - that marks the point of no return to life as you knew it.

THE - very fine line between life and "death."

Turning to look at John's face, I saw that he too understood the immense poignancy of this place.

John remained rooted to the spot where he was standing – his head moving as he surveyed each smiling face along the front line. His facial expression, telling everyone that he was not ready to cross over.

Silver Cloud broke the deafening silence. Turning to John, he told him that a bench would be placed at the end of the tunnel – a bench on which John could sit when he came to visit. The end of the tunnel, Silver Cloud explained, was a place to reflect, contemplate and make decisions – but most of all – it was a place filled with love, freedom and choice.

John acknowledged this information with a slight nod of his head. Looking towards the rows of spirit, we both bowed our heads in farewell, then John, Silver Cloud and I returned to serene comfort of the dimly lit ward.

John crossed the line a few short hours later at 3am on the 7th March.

I can tell you that John is now well, happy and pleased to be reunited with his family.

Healing into death can take many forms.
Each form – designed for the needs of the individual's higher self - at that particular moment in time.

Following the leadership of my Guides, when healing into death – I have played many different roles:

I play an active role - speaking words guided to me by Spirit.
I use music.
I use an Indian rattle.
I use crystals.
I use leaves and twigs.
Led by one Guide in particular – I used prayer.
Or –
I am a silent bystander.

The common factor that I have found – is that each of these roles has resulted in a peaceful "death."

What all these different roles tell me about ways of working with Spirit – and hopefully conveys to you – is:
There is no hard and fast, written in stone - "right" and "wrong" way. None of these roles is the "only" way.

For me – there is only "Their way."
All Guides are as different as each situation is – are as individual, as are we all, and it is for each of us, to find "the way" that works for our Guides and ourselves.

Crystals.

If you remember – I told you that Silver Cloud had asked me to hold a quartz crystal in my hand, before I travelled to Johns' bedside.

I had, in my collection – a few tumble stones – chosen for their colour – and one or two small pieces of quartz crystal. Quartz emits both, positive energy and has a cleansing property.

Although I loved my tumble stones and my quartz – I was an avid collector of rocks.
If I ever walk on a beach, it isn't long before I begin to fill my pockets – and John's pockets – with rocks and stones that I find "interesting".
I find "interesting" rock and stones on any land that I walk on. Some – I just stand and admire – some I find irresistible - a "must have" for my collection.

Since childhood - John has always been interested in crystals and fossils. In fact, much to his dad's annoyance - John used to dig large holes in the garden looking for hidden treasure. He once located a "lost" water pipe – the location of which turned out to be very useful information – when later the erection of a Garage was planned. All useful experience for a dowser.

As I related in detail in "More Friends Than You Know." - in 1994 – both John and I had had been psychically attacked, by a person who had programmed Quartz crystals in a negative way.
This person had used crystals – which he had given to us as a "gift" – to open a portal into our home, thus allowing his negative Spirit to visit, at will.

I found that episode very scary indeed – and initially I had a negative attitude towards crystals - not wanting any more in the house.
The positive outcome - was that I became aware of how powerful a crystal can be, and once I had rationalised - that it had been the person and not the crystal that had acted in a negative way – my fears began to subside.

About 3 months after we moved into the "warmest house that we have ever lived in" – John surprised me one day, by saying that he wanted to buy a few crystals. He explained that he wished to learn more about them and believed that they would help some of his patients. Still wary of the power of crystals and as bossy as ever – I replied "Ok – but keep them away from me."

Spirit – apparently – had a better idea.
On the day that John went to buy the crystals – Silver Cloud announced to me:
"You - will look after them."
This was not a request – but an order!

When John returned home and began to unpack the few crystals that he had bought – their positive, powerful energy began to fill the whole house. The energy was so strong – I was beginning to feel dizzy.

I dashed upstairs to the spare bedroom, where I knew some of my collection of rocks was. I collected two supermarket bags full of rocks – ran downstairs – and began to place the rocks in heaps around the room.
"What are you doing?" John asked in a bewildered manner. "The roof is lifting off the house – can't you feel it! I exclaimed.
"Yes I can feel their energy – it's great isn't it?"

"Honestly!" – I silently thought – "Silver Cloud is right – I'll have to look after these crystals – otherwise we'll both be on the ceiling."

So began our joint commitment to offer a supply of clean and positive crystals to people.
John eventually began to work with, and tutor - "crystal courses" – which are very popular – and I select the crystals that go on each course.
I ask the selection of crystals, "Who want's to go on this course?" – and the crystals volunteer or stay silent.
When the crystals return from an outing – they are all cleansed and put away till the next time.

One difference between John and I is - John knows and remembers, the names and properties of each crystal - I don't! (A phenomenon that was also reflected in our differing exam results at school!)

But what we have in common is - a "knowing".

We "know" when a crystal is right for someone – and we "know" when it isn't, and neither of us hesitates to express that opinion. Crystals are powerful tools – they hold ancient wisdom within their form.

They have the power to open chakras at will, and – as is the case of any healing practice - be that Spiritual healing – Crystal healing - Aromatherapy or Reiki etc – the practitioner has a duty to protect the recipient.

You see – John and I believe - that not only are we responsible for people on the courses - we are also responsible for the crystals that we choose to be the caretakers of.

I use crystals in my remote work with people and land when directed to - and my collection of rocks continues to grow.

Dowsing.

This will be a very short paragraph because basically – I was told by my first Guide – William - not to dowse.

"You'll be dowsing - dowsing - dowsing!" was his accusation.

I've narrated this story before – so I will not tell it again. Suffice to say – that William said this to me when he was beginning to teach me to communicate – therefore he quite rightly, diverted my attention away from my dabblings with dowsing.

However – with the communication that I receive from my Guides – I am able to locate both negative and positive lines, for example – with dowsing through my body – and then asking for their guidance.

Actually I am so talkative at times – that I ask too many questions of the pendulum – thus confusing myself.
This affliction of mine – asking questions – has got me in hot water with Spirit before.
My previous Doorkeeper – Buffalo – tiring of my constant questions, was forced to shout: *"ENOUGH – You must wait!"*

So – although I do own a couple of pendulums – and cherish my first one, which is a plastic, half chewed, apple core – that once adorned my neck in the 70s! – I prefer the communication approach.

Earth Energies and Land Clearance.

My work with land clearance is mainly done remotely.
With the communication from my Guides, and my ability to travel – I have found myself being taken on journeys through drains - and travelling underground like a worm. Drains are not my most favourite locations – but at least I don't get my Jeans dirty!

There are many diverse factors which can adversely affect land and buildings – and also - the people and animals that inhabit the land and buildings.
For example:
Ley lines.
Electricity cables and pylons.
Telephone masts.
The Earth's' own magnetic energy and gases.
Water: Streams, both on the surface and underground.
            Wells.
            Drainage water.
            Water tables – Rising or falling.
Spirit activity.
Demolition of buildings or parts thereof.

Erection of new buildings
Occupiers own negative energy and/or actions.
Earth Elementals.

So the key to a successful result, when approaching the healing of land and buildings – is definitely - to have an "open mind."

The solutions I have used and been witness to – are varied.
Always at the bequest of my Spirit guides: -
I have placed crystals in the ground to remove, or divert negative energy. I have "seen" energy barriers being erected – and have taken part in erecting them myself.
I have spoken with "earth elementals" who were angry at being disturbed by occupiers of the house.
I have grounded water courses and negative energy.
I have released Spirit from sites.

The solutions are as varied as the causes.

Spirit Release and Rescue.

Personally – I find this aspect of my work, one of the most rewarding. Firstly – The release of a Spirit entity which has been "trapped" in a house, building or on land – is a cause for celebration within the Spirit World. Secondly – To know and see - that the agitation, anger and distress of that entity are over – is reward in itself, and thirdly – Once the work has been completed - the relief of those people and animals in the physical world, who have been adversely affected by the presence of that entity – is almost tangible.

There are exceptions to the rule.

Not all Spirit who are attached to the Earth – wish to move on – or should be moved on, and attempts to interfere in their very existence – are futile and can result in further distress for all.

We all have free will – it is our given right.

Just as I discovered with the Monks from the Abbey: – Spirit has a right to continue their possession of the land that they inhabit. Who are we to tell them otherwise? But – as current inhabitors of the physical world – we have the right to ask for help – if we are fearful – sick – or unhappy.

Like everything in life – balance is the key to happiness.

I have spoken to Spirit – who have been frightened to leave the earth plane, frightened that the Spirit World would not welcome them because of a misdemeanour or crime they had committed. Frightened that loved ones would not, "wish to know" them. Frightened to come face to face with a parent, wife, husband – or ex husband, and frightened to leave loved ones behind.

Fear and self-recrimination – is a common finding.

I have witnessed Spirit – who in their cry for help, have caused mayhem in the physical world, sob with relief as they walked into the light with a "Guide" at their side.
I have also seen Spirit entities dragged back into the Spirit World – "escorted" by Angels in flowing gowns, and – in my experience - if Archangel Michael is in attendance – argument is futile!

Not everyone that requests help – realises that there is Spirit present in their house or place of work.

They will just report to me, that they are unwell – or feel uncomfortable in a certain room.

It is my job – to ask my Team for guidance.

Occasionally – when there is Spirit present - I am told by my team that we are not going to do the work ourselves. This is always exciting for me, because I know that the team are going ask the person who has requested the help – to perform the release or cleansing themselves. In these cases – my Team will pass step by step, precise instructions for me to pass on – and then the team and I "watch" from a distance.

This technique is used to help "nervous" or unsure budding channels – to overcome their nervousness and self doubt.

People have asked me to remove Spirit, who – I find - are only visiting, in order to give a message to that person. Invariably – I also find - during further conversation – that the message had been heard – but had been dismissed. Dismissed through self-disbelief or simply - not liking the message that was delivered.

I have been asked to remove a Spirit – only to discover that the person who has asked me – has themselves been asking for, "Spirit to come and visit me."

Having had their request answered – they have then been frightened by that very presence – or - they have unwittingly, invited a wandering pesky entity into their life that is revelling in its ability to frighten.

Asking for Spirit to visit – can be a wonderful experience – but be aware that an "open invitation" is just what it says it is.

Following a release, people report back to me:
They say how much "lighter" and "fresher" their dwelling feels and smells.
How – they now feel able to walk into the back bedroom – and how their children are sleeping in their own beds – all through the night. Those people who had been suffering from ailments (which can often be an ailment that the Spirit suffered from whilst in the physical life) – no longer have those symptoms, and – the biggest relief for them can be - that doors and drawers remain shut – no one walks on the stairs in the dead of night – or stands at the bottom of their bed.

I will end this topic with the story of the short stick and the rattling green crystal.

So, there I was – the day before I was due to visit a pub to release a Spirit - looking for a stick and a green crystal. The stick I had "seen" was short, (about 5 inches long) wooden, and was "turned" – like a table leg. This stick – I recognised – was the stick which was attached to the mini "warming pan" brass ornament – that had belonged to my mum.

I unpacked the box contained the ornament and proceeded to remove the "warming pan" – apologising to mum as the two items came apart. Having got the stick and the green crystal – I had to think of a way to attach them both together. Coming to my rescue – John suggested using a small glass bottle to hold the stone – and then attaching the bottle to the stick with insulation tape. I returned in triumph – from the kitchen holding a small roll of bright blue tape.

N.B.

It is my belief that every house should have a drawer in the kitchen that contains useful things. Things like: 3 odd screws, 6 assorted screwdrivers 1 packet of washers that don't fit anything, insulation tape, a squashed box of Elastoplast, and "something" sticky – all wound together by 3 feet of unravelled string.

Anyway – I digress.

With John's help – the crystal was placed in the bottle – which in turn was attached to the stick – by the blue tape. Relieved - that I had my rattling crystal attached to the stick - yet - bothered by its' very existence. What I would use it for, was beyond me!
Did they really expect me to walk round the pub with this in my hand? – I would look really stupid
The people at the pub would think I was weird!
Oh – it just wasn't fair!

Fortunately for me – because of the size of the stick – it fit into my handbag. Out of sight and hopefully – out of mind. I grasped onto the vain hope that - "They might even forget about it?"
Morning came, and John and I prepared to leave to drive to the pub. As we stepped outside onto the gravel drive – I noticed, amongst the grey stones of the gravel – a tiny blue stone. Strangely – for me – I didn't pick it up – but thought to myself – "I'll pick that up when we come back."

John and I had been at the pub for about half an hour – and after a warm welcome from the owners – and a cup of coffee and a chat – Silver Cloud told me to walk around to the back of the bar where I knew the Spirit was standing. This Spirit was Saxon – and had lived in the village where the pub was located.

He told me that he had happily chosen to live amongst the current inhabitants – but now he was sad:
Sad that everything he had known - had changed. Sad that he no longer felt that same "belonging" feeling, and sad that his presence - he knew - was upsetting a member of the bar staff. Yet, he was also sad – to leave:
He was uncertain that – given the length of time he had been apart from those of his era – there would be no one who he knew - waiting for him.

Silver Cloud reassured him that friends were waiting for him – and the Saxon said that he was happy to leave. I thought that my small part in this release would soon be finished.
Remaining on the floor, I listened as Silver Cloud explained that the Landlady was also sad.
She had grown accustomed to his presence – and were it not for the fact that a member of staff was becoming increasingly un-nerved by the Saxon – she would not have asked for our help.
I knew I needed to speak to her.

To my surprise – the landlady already thought that the Spirit could be Saxon – and she had given him a name.
I explained that he was now unhappy – and with a tear in her eye – she agreed that it would be best for him – to leave.

With everyone prepared – I returned to the bar.
"*You will need your rattle*" advised Silver Cloud.
"Oh no!" I thought as I spied my handbag on a table where I had left it. The owners of the bar were standing

by the table – watching – I had no choice but to walk to my handbag and retrieve the rattle – in full view!
I returned to the rear of the bar, and sat on the floor – holding the rattle in my hand.
The release was very quick and peaceful.

I returned to the table to return the rattle to my handbag. Noticing the rattle – the landlord asked: "What's that?" Embarrassed – I quickly explained the story of the rattle – including the finding of the blue stone. "A blue stone?" the landlord repeated – "I had one on the mantelpiece but it's disappeared."

When we returned home – the stone was still there in the gravel. I picked it up, took it indoors, and placed it on the mantelpiece.
Not long after – the stone disappeared!

Communication.

As I have described – my work with Spirit can involve the use of crystals, stones, music and twigs. I also use a Native American drum and rattle when working with earth energies, distant healing and occasionally – Spirit release. However – the constant factor – and for me the most precious of all tools – is the communication.
The communication that has been so accurate, up lifting, moving, informative, helpful, funny, and – where applicable – "painfully" honest

I am so grateful to be a communication channel.
Grateful to all those in Spirit who have come to speak to - and through me. Grateful to those in Spirit who continue to spend their precious time – teaching, guiding and protecting me. Grateful and priveledged to be able to continue working for and with them.

The last words of this piece are the words of Joseph, who, as I typed the heading "Communication" – came to give the following.

I leave you with his words.

> *"Communication is the lifeblood of all living things:*
> > *Animal - Vegetable – Mineral.*
>
> *What - and - How - we communicate to each other – predicts our combined destinies.*
>
> *Kind communication - combined with thoughtful action Heralds - a World at Peace."*

Joseph of Arimathaea - 6th February 2008.

CHAPTER ONE

WINGS ON MY FEET

My workroom in Garth was brilliant.

It was a large room on the first floor, which had been used as a sitting room, by the owners of the cottage. Through the windows – the views were of fields, trees and the far distant hills. The acoustics were also brilliant and well accommodated my love of loud music. The added bonus was that the sheep, who were our only neighbours, appeared to be undisturbed by the almost constant reverberating beat.

I began to indulge myself (with a vengeance) in spending a lot of time listening to, and using music.

For years, I had used music to alter my mood, used music to aid the lifting of my vibrations, and Spirit had used music to communicate with me.

Twelve busy months after the Bankruptcy – I now had the freedom to return to this favourite activity of mine.

It was heaven.

Using music also facilitated my travels with Silver Cloud, and on many occasions Silver Cloud, Wolf and I would travel down a river in a canoe – stopping to sit on the tiny beach, which looked out towards what I thought was an island.

On other occasions I was taken to a red, hot desert and was privileged to be in the company of other Native American Indians. On one such journey Silver Cloud and Wolf led me high up a mountain.

Standing on the top in the wind, the views far down below were tremendous and looking skyward - we saw an Eagle hovering on a current of air. Far below, I could still see the company of Natives going about their daily business and the far distant hills glimmered in the haze of the hot sun. Interrupting the awesome moment, Silver Cloud began to speak. He explained that I would be left on the top of the mountain on my own – adding - that as night fell and darkness encompassed me - I was to find my way down the mountain – where he and Wolf would be waiting. Silver Cloud and Wolf then left, walking back down the path that we had climbed.

Left on the hill – and waiting for nightfall – I sat crossed legged on the floor - watching and waiting as the sun slowly began to sink on the horizon.
The setting of the sun brought with it a chorus of strange sounds, both of insects and nocturnal animals.
Surrounded by these noises and now in complete darkness, I "asked" that I be given help to walk down into the valley below. Cautiously, I stood up and began my descent down the pathway – carefully placing one foot in front of the other. At first I stumbled on the stones that made up the pathway – and I asked for help once more. Although there was no light whatsoever – I found that when I looked down onto the path – I instinctively knew where the bigger, more hazardous stones were and could therefore avoid them.
I soon realised that if I just walked with Trust and Confidence – I would not stumble.

The journey down to meet Silver Cloud and Wolf, who were waiting as they said they would be, became easy.
However, once reunited with them and looking back up at the hill, which was now illuminated against a dawn sky – I saw how steep and craggy the mountain was.
I felt exhilarated. I felt a sense of achievement and I thanked those who had helped me.

I realised that with Trust and Confidence – anything could be achieved.

On another occasion, ten Shamans and myself sat in a cave to await and welcome the rising sun. This I knew – for them – was a daily ritual. For me – as I was invited to join them - I felt as though this was the first time I had performed the ritual, and yet – as the sun rose further into the sky, casting a thin ray of light onto the mouth of the cave – I felt as though I had done this many times before.

I feel that there is a very thin line between a "past life" experience and something, like the experience I have just described – in which I felt totally "at home", and so comfortable with – that it just feels "natural."

I try to live in the "Now" – and not look back.
I Am who I Am.

I Am however - very privileged to work with the American Indian – as I am privileged to work for all those in Spirit.

Not all these journeys were to the American desert.
On the 16th December 1997 – I was taken to Calvary – the place where Jesus was crucified.
Jesus was on the cross, his wrists and feet nailed, his head slumped down.
As I looked at him, I said out loud, "Jesus was a Shaman." As the words left my mouth – Jesus held his head upright, smiled, and jumped down off the cross. He stood still, rubbing his hands together as if anticipating a forthcoming, exciting event.
We grinned at each other.

Then - in a jaunty manner – he turned and walked away.

Not all the journeys were with Silver Cloud.
I had also met Joseph of Arimathaea.
Joseph showed me views of the planets.
He took me to Africa, Australia, China, Russia, Europe, North and South America and Canada.
On each continent I would experience its own unique vibration. They were wondrous trips.

On Christmas day 1997, John and I were visited by our families in Spirit. They brought with them a specially prepared plank of wood – on which was painted the words – "Merry Christmas."

Just after Christmas, I rang our two friends in America – Joy and Sandra.
During that conversation and "out of the blue" – Sandra asked me – "Why aren't you over here?"
Surprised and confused, and not knowing how to answer her I just replied with a little laugh.
"I'm serious." She continued – "Why aren't you over here? It would be lovely to meet you. Come and stay with us. May would be a good month."

I was, if you'll pardon the phrase – "Gobsmacked."
I was totally lost for words, as loads of thoughts tumbled through my mind in a matter of seconds.

My first thought was that – Joy, Sandra and I, had never met – "Why would they want to invite a virtual

stranger to stay with them. Yes – we got on together – over the phone – but what would happen if I got on their nerves!"
Then other thoughts followed:
I had never visited any other country! - I'd only been to Cornwall twice!
I couldn't possibly fly in an aeroplane!!
I couldn't go to America! - Flying, was what other people did?
How much did it cost?
What clothes do you wear in Arizona?
Where was Arizona?
Jack and Jill (our two border collies) would miss me – I would miss Jack and Jill.
John would live on beans on toast!
Is the sky really that blue?
Is the sand really so red?

Thanks but No – you'd never get me on an aeroplane.
I don't like heights - I would have to be sick in one of those little paper bags!!

Over the next few days - the shock and suddenness of the invitation sent me scurrying to my work room. I lost myself in my Enya CD – "Paint the Sky with Stars."
Time in my room also meant that I could avoid any questions from John. Questions like – "What do you think about Joy and Sandra's invitation?"

I hadn't been able to stop thinking about it – try as I might.
The prospect was too daunting to contemplate and yet – the prospect was really exciting.

On the morning of the 30th December 1997, Silver Cloud and I were standing on top of a cloud – as you do

– and a tree rose up out of it. I walked over to the tree (clouds are remarkably sturdy underfoot) and noticed that there were pieces of paper dangling off its branches. I chose a piece of paper and plucked it off a branch. There was a word written on it – that word was – *Love.*

A silver ladder now rose up through the cloud and I knew that was my cue to leave.

Thanking Silver Cloud – I stepped onto the ladder and climbed back down through the cloud.

Wolf was waiting for me as I stepped off the bottom rung.

As I looked at him, I knew that I was surrounded by the love of Spirit – and - I realised - that love had brought the invitation from Arizona?

The next day – New Years Eve – Silver Cloud and I travelled in his canoe – down that now familiar river. We arrived at an Indian village where we both went to greet - and be greeted by - the Indians who were present.

This greeting took the form of - hands held flat together, in a prayer like manner and brought up towards the face – followed by a slight bow and nod of the head, much in the style of an Asian Indian greeting.

A conversation began between us – and as so often happens – as I lower my vibrations some time later – I cannot recall all that has been said.

This phenomena used to really annoy me – but understanding that – on some higher level of consciousness – I can recall it - I have learned to be grateful and gracious for all the communication I receive whether I can recall it or not.

On the 3rd of January Silver Cloud took me down "our" river once more.

We stopped by the small sandy beach.

Climbing out of the canoe, we paddled through the shallow water, and made our way along the beach – where we sat down in the sunny spot.

I noticed that my bare wet legs now had sand stuck to them – but as we sat in the hot sunshine the sand dried and fell away.

To my delight – Buffalo and Armon came walking down the path to my right – they sat down with Silver Cloud and I.

(Buffalo, I remind you, had been my doorkeeper prior to Wolf - he had left to work as a Guide. Armon is my mothers' brother. Uncle Armon, had died in 1945 and has been a companion and mentor of mine since I was a baby).

We three spent a short time together in contented silence, and as Armon and Buffalo left to walk back down the narrow path – I noticed a pile of fir cones lying near to me.

Reaching towards them, I picked up one of the closed cones and held it in the palm of my hand.

The cone opened and released its seeds, which fell away onto the ground.

"They are seeds of new beginnings", said Silver Cloud.

I understood the message of Silver Clouds words as
I was still contemplating the prospect of travelling to Arizona. Still making endless lists in my head, of all the "pros" and "cons", endlessly asking myself if I could pluck up the courage to say "yes." Still asking myself if I was brave enough to step into the unknown.

Knowing that I needed time to ponder on my dilemma – Silver Cloud dismissed me. Standing up, he said - *"Time to go."*
I said "Goodbye" to Silver Cloud and Wolf appeared by my side to escort me safely "back to my chair."
(For those of you who haven't heard me use this phrase before – it means that I lowered my vibrations and grounded myself. This procedure ends all my trips with Spirit and every communication session).

The same question kept circling around my head - "would I be able to step on an aeroplane – on my own?"
I was 46yrs old and the nearest I had ever got to an aeroplane had been visits to Manchester Airport.
When we were in our late teens/early twenties – John and I would drive to Manchester airport on summer evenings. At that time - the public were allowed to stand on the roof of the Terminal building to watch the incoming and outgoing flights. We would stand and watch the passengers stepping off the incoming flights and have a competition between us – wanting to be the first to spot the straw donkey wearing a Sombrero!

I had always looked forward to these trips and was fascinated by all the comings and goings – but – my stomach lurched as I watched the planes take off I had always said, "You'd never get me on one of those."

Now – here I was, contemplating that very thing!

Contemplating what I would wear - IF I went?
Wondering if I would be sick on the plane – IF I went?
Wondering if I would discover that I was claustrophobic, which, when added to my fear of

heights – would result in sedation – as the cabin crew wrestled with my ranting and raving body?

Wondering what the sky looked like – at 30.000 ft?
Wondering - what it would be like to step foot on American soil?

John had already assured me that we would find the money for the airfare – he had already visited a Travel agent and been given some approximate figures, and he was thrilled that I had been given such a brilliant opportunity. I knew that he would have no hesitation in accepting Joy and Sandra's' invitation - and I wished that I could be like him.

But I was still dithering – still daunted - by what was for me – the enormity of such a journey.
Silver Cloud was, I know – gently nudging me to accept the invitation, and Joy and Sandra were still awaiting my answer!

In mid January – John asked me THE question that I had been dreading - and had avoided asking myself.

"Well – are you going to go - or not?"

Sitting in my chair, I avoided looking at him.
After a couple of seconds – and knowing that there would be no going back on my decision – I took a deep breath and replied:
"YES. – I'm going to go to Arizona."
"Oh my god" I squealed, "I'm going to Arizona!!"
I was so excited and relieved at my decision – now - I thought to myself – "All I have to do is get there!"

Being a smoker and having decided to accept Joy and Sandra's invitation, my immediate thoughts turned to prospect of what I knew would be an 8hr flight.

I know – I thought - "I'll get one of those 'Smoking tickets' – Like I saw on that comedy film – Airplane."

In my minds eye – I saw the scene in which a passenger, booking onto a flight was asked – "Smoking or Non Smoking?" "Smoking" he answered.

The passenger was then handed a boarding pass that was on fire.

Well – it was funny at the time!

"So - I'll be fine?" I reassured myself – "As long as I can have my cigarettes!"

I wasted no time in rushing to the telephone to ring Joy and Sandra. I was very eager to accept their generous invitation.

When the telephone was answered, I announced excitedly, "Hi, its Lynn."

I was a little dismayed to hear a subdued Joy on the other end.

Maybe they had changed their minds? I thought.

Panicking, I asked – "Do you still want me to come? Have you changed your minds?"

Joy replied – "Do you know what time it is over here? It's 5am!"

I was mortified and in a rush of embarrassment, I blurted out:

"Oh, I'm sorry. I'll go - Sorry – I'm really sorry – I'll ring you later shall I? – Sorry – I just wanted to tell you that I am coming."

"Good - Give us a ring when you have some details" came the sleepy answer.

February took me into the previously unknown world of passport photographs and travel arrangements.

The lady at the Travel Agents was very kind and helpful. She – in the knowledge that I was a solo - first time flyer – carefully explained that I would be flying from Manchester to Chicago, (an 8hr flight) where I would catch ANOTHER aeroplane to Phoenix, Arizona. (I think that was a 3 to 4hr flight)

Oh – and by the way – she added - "Smoking is not allowed!"

There was to be no "smoking ticket"! Panic began to set in – "How could I do all that travelling without my cigarettes?

Sitting in her office and following my itinerary on the paper work that was spread out on her desk – I was relieved to find myself, quickly and with no hold ups - in Phoenix.

She then suggested that I telephone my friends – to ask them if they would meet me in Phoenix - or would I then have to travel onto Sedona myself?

I hadn't thought of that!
Don't tell me I would have to get on another aeroplane!

I was trying to work out just how long I would have to be in the air – but the differing American Time Zones, completely blew my mind. I found it impossible to calculate it all and the words of Silver Cloud came back to me – *"Why do you have to plan everything?"*

My answer had always been – "Because I need to know." Now – I was beginning to realise that actually – "I didn't need to know – if the lady in the travel Agents – who was used to travelling herself – said it would work – then work it would."

11

I was however, a little unnerved when she smiled and said – "and of course – once you check your suitcase in at Manchester Airport – you won't see it again until you land in Phoenix."

AHH! My clothes!!

With the basic flight details in place, and the departure date provisionally booked for the 25th May – returning on the 4th June - I carefully calculated the 7hr time difference between Sedona and North Wales.

Satisfying myself it was past 10am in Sedona – I picked up the telephone and dialled Joy and Sandra's telephone number.

The dates were acceptable for them and they too, seemed as excited as I was - that we were going to meet at last. I said – "If you get fed up with me, point me in the direction of a bed and breakfast." "That's easy", was the reply – there's a Motel just down the road."

With bated breath I asked – "How do I get from Phoenix to Sedona?"

"Oh – that's easy too" said Joy – "You get the Shuttle." With my mind conjuring pictures of rockets or tiny two seater aeroplanes, I asked, "What's the shuttle?" "It's a mini bus. The company is based at Phoenix Airport and the drive takes 2hrs. We'll give you the telephone number to ring."

My only experience of minibuses had been those Ford Transit vans that John and I had hired when we'd been clearing rubbish or moving house. Those vans has been very uncomfortable, and there had been one famous occasion when we had driven about fifty miles in one particularly rickety one. When we reached our destination and alighted from the van – we discovered that all feeling had been lost from our legs - neither of us could walk in a straight line. Our plight caused much amusement - not only to ourselves – but also to those who witnessed us staggering across the car park.

Based on that passed experience, the idea of a 2hr drive in a mini bus, following the two fights, was not one that I relished. The forthcoming journey was beginning to feel - never ending and somewhat gruelsome and having heard people talk of the dreaded "jet lag" – I asked my team to assist me on the journey so that I could enjoy all of this spectacular holiday.

With the flights and the shuttle booked - and on the advice of my sister in law, to – "fly in a pair of shoes that allowed for any swelling of your feet" – I bought a pair of reddy/orange Moccasin shoes – my "Arizona" shoes.
Now all I had to do was wait for the 25th to arrive.

Whilst waiting, I continued to spend time in my workroom listening to music.
As I mentioned earlier, I had been listening to Enya's album, "Paint the Sky with Stars."
One track in particular was especially poignant and I had listened to it repeatedly:

Track 5 - "Only If" The chorus of which is:

"If you really want to, you can hear me say.
Only if you want to, will you find a way.
If you really want to, you can seize the day.
Only if you want to, will you fly away."

Whilst listening to music on the 13th March I was "grounded" by an unknown Spirit.

I "returned to my chair" full of excitement and impatience – impatience for my journey to begin.
I just wanted to pack my case and go!

The previous day, a friend had visited and suddenly asked me if I was writing a book. I knew that she was referring to the book "More Friends Than You Know."
"No" I replied, "I'm not writing it yet."

"My Guides are telling me - to tell you - that you must put your notes in your room."
John joined in the conversation saying that he agreed and that I should get all my notes together.
Feeling under pressure – I agreed that I would.

Following this conversation, and on the 15th March – I got all my notebooks out and put them in my room. John moved a small, old computer onto a table in the corner of my room and I was all set to go.

However – I had no experience of computers at all so I wrote the instructions of how to switch it on and off – onto a piece of paper, and with those basic instructions I sat down and began to type that very afternoon.

I wrote every day and into the night. That is, until the 5th April, when – horror of horrors – the computer ate my book!
With one careless press of a button it had taken me less than a nanno second - to prove that the "idiot proof" computer – wasn't.
John was away, and when he came home the next day, he tried everything to retrieve the book – but to no

avail. The computer refused to reveal its whereabouts and John reluctantly told me that the book had vanished.

I was devastated.
I took it all very personally and found that I couldn't return to my room for a period of 2 weeks.
Eight years later – in February 2006 – I began the book again. This time I was much more organised and keen to fulfil "their" wish, and as I was writing it – guess what? – the original effort turned up on a floppy disc.
Neither of us knows how this happened – but we think we know a man who does!!

But – back to the 26th March 1998.

I "raised my vibrations" and Peter, a Spirit from the Alien World was waiting to speak. He communicated the following verses:

Peter.

"Tomorrow will come.
Search today, to find the things we wish for tomorrow.
Yesterday will be too late – as we will have lost today.

Almighty winds bear our wishes for the future.
Rushing water takes our pain away.
The sun brings joy – and lifts us upwards – to catch the mighty wind of hope."

"Many times – we live
Many times – we die.
But the one certainty is that – many times we must
endure.
Therefore – we must plan for our future.
Plan to sustain life in all forms.
For tomorrow – it is us who will return.

Trust yourself – for within is the answer.
Outside forces call – Who and from Where?
Where and What to believe?
Truth is the answer.
But the Only Truth – is your Own."

10th April 1998. Good Friday.

Joseph of Aramathaea was by my side as I "raised my vibrations" and went into a meditation.

During the meditation I regressed into my mothers womb. From that starting point – I advanced through certain ages - reliving certain events.

As I arrived back to the present day – I discovered that my body was encumbered with chains.

Joseph handed me a pair of bolt cutters. I knew that now was my chance to cut those chains that restricted me - and that I felt restricted by.

I began to release the binds.

As I finished – I was "grounded", and a small pair of white feathery wings were fitted to my feet.

It was a very moving and uplifting experience. An experience which ended with words from Silver Cloud:
"*You have chosen.*
And you have chosen your life's' work."

25th May 1998.

It was 6am on a grey drizzly, Monday morning.
My suitcase - bedecked with two turquoise ribbons and two stick-on red dragons – for identification purposes - was in the boot of the car. In my hand I held a rucksack, which was my hand luggage.
Before getting into the car, I glanced back at the cottage. Jack and Jill had raced down to the room at the end of the house, and were now sitting on a blanket chest and watching out of the window. With tears stinging my eyes, I muttered – "Won't be long you two."

With my "Arizona" shoes on my feet – John and I got into the car and began the journey to Manchester airport.
Normally a chatty passenger – the early hour - the mix of fear and excitement – and the vision of those two faces at the window - silenced me.
As we were travelling along the M56 and as the "airport" signs came into view I began to wonder - "Why? - was it necessary to be at the Airport 3 hrs before the flight departure?"
Three hours in which my nerves would jangle and twist – "Were there plenty of toilets?" "Where could I have a cigarette?" Did I pack my passport?" "Was there enough food in the house for John, Jack and Jill?"
"Did the airport know I was coming?"

The hour and a half drive to the airport passed slowly and then all at once – the airport buildings came into view. From behind the buildings a departing aeroplane soared into the sky – "Oh my God!" I thought, "It's a miracle that something so big can just – well – fly."
The sight of that plane as it soared into the sky made me gasp. I hurriedly asked Silver Cloud and Wolf to protect me – "Pleease!"

Having parked the car, I was standing in the rain having a cigarette as John calmly went to retrieve my suitcase from the boot.
Waiting patiently for me to finish the cigarette – he smiled and said – "Right – are you ready to go in?"
I looked towards the Terminal building, took a breath in and exhaled slowly – "Right – I'm ready" I replied. Anyone would have thought I was going into battle. "It's just an aeroplane" I said to myself – "Thousands of people fly every day."
John loves flying. His days working as a photographer had given him the opportunity to fly in small Cessna aircraft, gliders and helicopters, hanging out of their windows and doorways – in order to take Aerial views. In fact – as far as John is concerned – "the smaller the better."
For my first attempt – I wanted a "Big One."

The airport was busy as we walked over to the checkin desk. John ushered me into the correct queue and we waited until it was our turn. I say our, because up until this point, John never left my side. But when we walked up to the desk and I handed my ticket and passport - (that I had proudly encased in a leather holder – which was a gift from my sister) - over to the smiling lady, she asked him, "Are you flying sir?"

John explained that, "No" he wasn't flying – but as I had never flown before he was helping me.

"Right" she continued – "Would you stand to one side please."

As he moved away the smiling lady picked up my ticket and began to question me.

You'll no doubt know the questions they ask:

"Have you packed your own bags?"

"Has anyone asked you to take a package for them?"

I answered her questions with the same amount of solemnness in which they were asked, and before I had time to think – my suitcase was swiftly placed onto a conveyor belt, and disappeared out of view.

AAH! - My clothes – my Factor 30!

Thankfully – I had put my little travelling companion, a tiny bear called Yorrick, in my hand luggage – ensuring that at least he and I would arrive in Chicago together!

John had suggested that I ask for a window seat and my request had been granted. So – with my boarding pass and my passport held tightly in my hand – I returned to join John – "Have I got time to go outside for another cigarette?" I asked him. "Yes" came the reply – "You've got just under 3 hrs to wait now."

"Oh dear!" I thought, "That is an awful long time – I don't know if my nerves will stand the waiting?"

Two cups of coffee and four trips to the Ladies later – John said that if I wanted time to visit the "Duty Free" shop, as I had mentioned, he thought it was time for me to go through to Departures.

This was a really strange moment for John and I.

We were both used to John going away, but I always stayed at home with Jack and Jill. In fact I had never been apart from them and they were 3yrs old now.

The memory of their faces at the window as we had left that morning made my cry.

John walked me over to the entrance to Departures, and I couldn't hold back the tears.
I knew that once I walked through those doors – I would be on my own, well - physically at least.

I didn't know what to expect during this trip.
But – I did know that this was a brilliant opportunity.
So, with tears running silently down my face and with one last wave, to a smiling John - my Arizona shoes and I walked through into Departures.

I followed the signs and found my way to Duty Free where I purchased some cigarettes. As I was placing them in my hand luggage I spotted Yorricks little face peering up at me. Thinking that he looked a little bewildered, I realised that - far from being on my own – I was responsible for this little character - who was also travelling into the unknown. "Don't worry" I reassured him "I'll look after you."
My nervousness eased.
Feeling responsible for Yorrick diverted the nervous tension away from myself - after all – "I was the adult wasn't I?"

Having successfully negotiated my way through Duty Free I then followed the signs, which led me to my "gate."
There were plenty of seats available so I sat myself down. After checking that I still had my boarding pass and passport near to hand, I picked up my rucksack and walked towards a huge window. Speaking to Yorrick – I said, "let's go and look through the window."

On the tarmac below me stood a large, silver aeroplane with the letters AA painted on the fuselage, the letters were red and blue in colour.

American Airlines! This must be my plane!

It was huge!

I looked in wonder at the sight – "Look Yorrick – our plane."

I was so excited to see the plane I wanted to share the vision with John. Looking about me, I spotted a public telephone on the wall. "I know – I'll ring and leave him a message on the Answerphone."

Dialling our home number the Answerphone picked up. "Hi – it's me. Just wanted to let you know that I'm OK. Guess what – I've just seen my plane! It's a great big silver one – its brilliant!"

Finishing the conversation I placed the handset back into the cradle. As I turned round I nearly fell over the feet of a middle-aged couple who had sat in two seats by the telephone; they were grinning at me. I realised that they must have heard all my conversation and witnessed my childish excitement.

Gathering my compose, and saying to myself – "Trust and Confidence Lynn" - I smiled at them and made an effort to walk away in a confident, dignified manner. Trying to give the impression to the other waiting passengers - that I was used to sitting around Departure lounges, trying to give the impression that I was a "frequent flyer", and trying to contain my excitement.

More people began to gather at the gate and after what seemed like an awful long wait the airline staff appeared.

I quickly dashed off to the toilet – again!

John had warned me that the staff would call for the passengers to board in blocks of seat numbers, so I sat down and listened intently as the numbers were called out.

Hearing my number called – I picked up my rucksack and said to Yorrick, "That's us Yorrick – time to get on the plane."

Stepping through the doorway and onto the aircraft, I turned to my right, as indicated by a member of the cabin crew. Clutching my boarding pass in my hand, with its all important seat number printed on it - I was very pleasantly surprised by the comfortable looking seats, with lots of leg-room. "Oh this will be great" I thought. However, the line of people in front of me just kept moving along, so I followed.

We stepped through another doorway, and the general atmosphere turned a little darker. The seats – I noticed – were closer together, the leg room more confined, and there were rows and rows of them. It was then, that I realised - we had entered the plane through the First Class section!

"Maybe I will have a row to myself?" I pondered.

I found my window seat, sat down and quickly put my seat belt on. Fifteen minutes later, people were still walking up the isle – but still no one sat in the seat next to mine. Just as I was beginning to think that there would be an empty seat next to me – a man stopped, put his bag in the overhead locker and sat himself down in the next seat.

We smiled at each other and slowly a conversation began. Firstly we spoke about the wet Manchester weather and how lucky we were to be leaving it behind, then the conversation turned to our respective, final destinations and length of stay.

By now, the cabin crew had shut the doors to the aeroplane and I heard the engines of the plane.

Clutching my hand over my seat belt, I thought – "I don't know if I can do this? – If I don't get off now, it will be too late."

Turning to the friendly man beside me I said – "I haven't flown before."

"Oh, you'll' love it" he assured me - "Once we get through the clouds, you'll have a lovely view through the window."

Anticipating the lovely view – I sat back and tried to relax.

The aeroplane began to move backwards and then turned to make its slow journey to the end of the runway.

Silently, I spoke to Yorrick, who was still in my rucksack, which I had stowed under my seat, "We're moving now Yorrick."

John had told me that he would leave the airport and drive to an open vantage point, from which he could watch the plane take off.

As the plane came to a halt at what I presumed was the end of the runway, my fellow passenger explained that we would remain stationary until the pilot was given clearance for take off.

As we sat waiting, I silently spoke to John, "I'm OK – there's a nice man sat next to me, Bye John, Bye. Bye Jack and Jill."

The nice man – I never knew his name – leant towards me and said, "As the plane gathers speed – you will feel the plane judder – that's perfectly normal."

I was grateful for his warning, as the plane did indeed judder. Were it not for his warning, I might have panicked, instead – I was able to sit back and enjoy the thrill of leaving the ground behind and soaring into the sky! It was brilliant!

"Bye John."

"Bye Jack and Jill."

"Bye England."

Garth Cottage

View of the hills from Garth

Our nearest neighbour

Christmas 1997

John and Jack

Jack (left) and Jill in the garden at Garth

Joy (left) and Sandra

Jack and Jill watching through the window

"My" aeroplane at Manchester Airport

CHAPTER TWO

SPIRITS FLY HIGH

I quickly discovered that I loved flying. "Why?" I mused, "Had I never flown before?" The answer came to me, "Because there had never been anywhere I had wanted to travel to – until Arizona."

The whole flight was wonderful.
The views of the blue sky, from out of my little window, were fantastic.
My fellow passenger informed me of the imminent arrival of the refreshment trolley, (he had done this trip many times) – and when the hot towels were brought round – his advise to use them – was very good advice indeed.
When I left my seat to visit the toilet - his warning about the noisy flush system – still didn't prepare me for the gushing sound that reverberated within that small space. And for a split second, I thought I had pushed the wrong button. I braced myself against the walls of that confined space – expecting the plane to nose dive towards the ground.
Recovering my composure, I returned to my seat, smiled and said, as casually as I could – "You were right about that toilet."

One of the things that I had been looking forward to on this flight – was the sound of American accents.
Given that I was travelling on American Airlines the first American accents I heard were those of the boarding staff. Hearing these accents really enforced the thrill that I now felt – the thrill of visiting another country.

I anticipated that – just as I had seen on many American films that I had watched on the television – the cabin crew would be constantly saying – "You're welcome" – "Enjoy your flight" and "Have a nice daaay." I also thought that every American had very white teeth!

I have to say that the cabin crew on this particular flight was consistently downbeat – which I found disappointing.
However – as the refreshment trolley came along – my spirit was revived with the offer of a cup of tea.
As the male steward handed the cup of tea over to me and I thanked him – he replied – "You're welcome."

"Great!" I thought to myself – "America here I come!"

As I drank my cup of American tea – my thoughts drifted to the contents of my suitcase (which hopefully was in the hold). In particular - I pictured the box of tea bags that I had packed – and I hoped that the box contained enough tea to last for the entire 11-day duration of my trip!

I was fascinated with the views out of the window.
The blue sky and fluffy clouds were a wonder to behold – and the land far below – mesmerised me.
One part of this journey that had bothered me a few weeks ago – had been the knowledge that we would be flying over water.
I can't swim!
But as we left the land behind us, and the water came into view – I could see the sun sparkling on its surface – the tips of the tiny waves, resembling the twinkling stars on a cold frosty night.
Every view through that window fascinated me.

The long 8hr flight was interrupted by the very welcome refreshment trolley and the food.

I can't remember what we had to eat – but the whole experience was exciting and new to me, and I was loving every minute of it.

As we neared Chicago airport – the friendly passenger reminded me to alter my watch to the Chicago time line and then began to describe the views of the City outline. He mentioned the names of some of the buildings that we would see and I got very excited as we began our decent into O'Hare airport.

However, the mist obscured the apparently "normal" views.

To be honest with you – after 8 hrs, chewing gum to curb my nicotine withdrawal (it didn't work!) – the knowledge that soon I would be able to have a cigarette quelled my disappointment and as the plane came in to land – my Arizona shoes were itching to stand on American soil whilst I fed my habit.

The landing at Chicago airport was equally as exciting as the taking off had been and once again, my fellow passenger told me what to expect. His information allowed me to relax and I fixed my gaze through the window. I watched, as the land below loomed ever closer and I tried to estimate the exact time when the wheels of the plane would touch down. I sat back in my seat as the brakes of the aircraft were applied and wallowed in the energy as the brakes slowed the plane down.

As the plane slowly moved towards the gate – I took the opportunity to thank the man for all the help he had given me. I felt so fortunate to have been in his company – he had helped to make my first flight a truly brilliant experience.

He, in turn, said that he had enjoyed chatting to me and we both agreed that it had indeed, been a very enjoyable flight.

I silently – thanked Wolf and Silver Cloud for all their help in this matter, adding – "Are you happy to be back home?"

I received no answer, but assumed that they were just as excited as me to continue on this journey of ours.

The Travel Agent had arranged for a "meeter and greeter" to meet me – but as I gazed around arrivals I could see that there was no one was standing, holding a board with my name written on it - which is what I had been told to expect.

As I stood gazing around feeling unsure what to do - once again my fellow passenger came to my rescue. He escorted me towards the customs desks, where we both stood in line – in fact – we were the first in the queue.

The stern looking male officer beckoned me forward.

Smiling, I approached the desk.

My smile was not reciprocated and the officer began to ask his questions.

"Where are you travelling to?"

"Where are you staying?"

And – "What is the duration of your stay?"

 It was at this point that I realised that - actually – I didn't know where Joy and Sandra lived in Sedona – I only had their telephone number and PO Box number.

Hastily – I scrambled around in my rucksack for the little blue book in which these scant details were written.

My duty free cigarettes began to cascade over the rim of my bag and Yorrick popped his head up to say "hello" to the "nice" man.

Finding the book and my travel documents – I handed them all to the officer, who studied them with a un-nerving intensity.

After what seemed a lifetime – the officer handed all the documents back to me.

Un-smiling – he said, "Enjoy your stay."

Relieved that the Americans were going to allow me into their country, I was dismayed that he hadn't stamped my passport. Taking a deep breath I asked:

"Could you please stamp my passport? This is my first ever flight – and it would be brilliant if you could stamp my passport."

I slid the passport back towards him. After a couple of seconds – he simultainiously reached for the passport with one hand and grasped a rubber stamp with the other.

"I think I can manage that." He said.

With one movement – the passport was opened, stamped, and slid back towards me.

I even glimpsed a hint of a smile as he said the words:

"Have a nice daaay."

Picking my passport up – I smiled and thanked him.

"Next" – he shouted.

My fellow passenger was behind me in the queue and so I walked between the line of customs desks and stepped into the terminal. My intention was to wait until the passenger came through customs where I would thank him once again.

I stood with my back to the desks – absorbing the activity around me. A convoy of cages containing suitcases was driven through the doors to my left and I scanned the cages – wondering if my suitcase was amongst them. I didn't see it.

Remembering the passenger – I turned back towards the customs desk. The queues were now quite long – but to my dismay – there was no sign of him.

I quickly looked round the immediate area – but the passenger had vanished.

I remain very grateful to him for all the care he showed to me throughout that flight. He helped to make my maiden voyage a very happy and relaxed one.

Standing there in the midst of all the noisy activity, I felt alone.

Talking to myself – I asked; "Right Lynn – what do you need to do now?" Knowing that I had plenty of time to find the boarding gate for Phoenix – I replied - "Have a cigarette."

Remembering that the travel agent had said that I would be able to smoke outside the terminal building – I followed the Exit signs.

The heat was the first thing that greeted me as I stepped outside the building. I had never experienced such a high temperature. My thoughts went once again to my suitcase – had I brought the right clothes? – my jeans would probably stay in the case?

Drifting towards a small group of smokers who had gathered around a waste bin – I stood listening to the sounds around me. Car horns and the constant hum of traffic – interspersed with the sound of distant police sirens were the sounds that met my ears.

But the sight that fascinated me was the constant stream of stretched white limousines that stopped to fleetingly disgorge its passengers and their luggage and then speed off again – only to be replaced by another one.

Chicago airport is a very large airport and I discovered that in order to catch my flight to Phoenix, I would have to be transported to the other side of the concourse - via Monorail.

If I had been given the opportunity to get on a Monorail back in England, I would have said "No thankyou." But there was no choice – so I explained to Yorrick what we would be doing. The staff were all very helpful, so myself and other passengers – who were also destined for the same terminal – were gently herded onto the monorail.

The monorail felt safe and secure and the trip to the next terminal allowed for a sight seeing tour of the airport that I hadn't expected.

Arriving at the terminal and still with plenty of time to check in – I once more joined a group of fellow smokers who were standing outside the building.

Using my new found skill of following overhead signs and little arrows – I soon found my way to the check in desk. Relieved, when the assistant found my name on the flight list, my confidence began to grow. Once again I asked for a window seat and my request was granted.

I had told John that I would try to ring him from Chicago and looking round – I saw a row of public telephones.

I reached into my rucksack to find my little blue book. Ever prepared – I had written the international number for England on its back page.

I dialled the number and waited. Hearing no sound down the line – I dialled again.

Still the phone did not ring.

I replaced the phone in its cradle and looked around me.

Standing within arms length, was a young man and I asked him if he could help me. He was very obliging and having tried the number I showed him himself, he rang the international operator for me. Very quickly, I heard a telephone ringing.

John answered and I hastily told him that I had arrived in Chicago - a young man had helped me with the telephone - and that I had checked in for my flight to Phoenix and was standing right by the gate.

It was difficult to hear John's response with all the public announcements and the conversations of the passengers who were also waiting for the same flight – but I was great to speak to him and let him know that I was OK – as I knew he would be wondering. And it was great to hear that he was OK – as were Jack and Jill.

After I put the telephone receiver down, a public address announcement come over the tannoy. "The gate," it said, "for passengers to Phoenix has been changed."

I don't remember the exact gate numbers, but it was something like gate 96 to gate 43. A mad scramble for hand luggage ensued and as everyone else but me - seemed to know where they were going - I followed them.

The walk to the new gate seemed endless and I carefully read the overhead signs to ensure that I was going in the right direction. Periodically glancing at my watch watching the seconds go by - I hoped that I would arrive at the new gate in time.

Arriving at the new gate – I joined the queue to check in again – only to find that the computer at the last check in had done its' job and I and my seat allocation were already on the list.

The flight to Phoenix was fascinating – as through my window I had my first real views of America.

When the refreshments came around I used the opportunity to strike up a conversation with the lady who was sitting in the next seat to me.

Disappointingly – she didn't appear to be interested in the fact that I had flown from Manchester, England on my maiden flight and had been awake for many hours – a feat that I thought worth mentioning.

However she did wish me a "nice staaay" and smiled sweetly – a smile that indicated the end of the conversation.

Another landing later - and yet another time zone entered - I arrived in Phoenix Arizona.

To my relief - my suitcase was also in Phoenix Arizona.

Having made a few enquiries in the terminal – I made my way to the shuttle bus desk – which to my delight, was situated on the very outskirts of the terminal – allowing easy access to the outside.

Having confirmed my booking with the lady at the desk and leaving my suitcase with her, I wandered outside for a cigarette.

The sun was even hotter in Phoenix than it had been in Chicago, the heat rising up from the pavement (or should I say – sidewalk) through my Arizona shoes.

I had felt the heat of this land when I had travelled with Silver Cloud – but it was a joy to actually physically stand there. The accents, the white limousines, the vastness of the buildings and the heat - told me that I really was – in America.

Having the time now to gather my thoughts - I have to say that I also felt a sense of achievement as I stood on that pavement. And in a strange way, although I didn't quite understand why - I felt as though I was giving something back to Buffalo, Wolf, Silver Cloud and his Guide, White Cloud.

And – the shuttle bus – was a very posh bus indeed! With its large comfortable seats, air conditioning and very hospitable driver – it was nothing like the transit vans that John and I had hired.

Sitting in the bus with my fellow passengers I realised that I was the only English person. For the first time in my life I was the foreigner and momentarily - that felt very strange.

Sitting with my fellow passengers in the shuttle bus – we headed out of Phoenix.

I was struck by the vastness of the road along which we travelled – and was also surprised at the seemingly sedate pace that we were travelling. I had always thought that Americans lived in the "fast lane." But this speed felt very slow when compared to the M6 back home.

As we travelled through the outskirts of Phoenix, dusk began to fall. Suddenly – out of the gloom I spied - a cactus! Then another – then another!

Resisting the urge to turn to the lady sitting near me and point the cactus out to her I silently spoke to Yorrick and John:

"A cactus! We must be in the desert now Yorrick! Are you excited?"

"John – I've just seen a cactus!"

We drove on through the darkness and eventually the shuttle bus glided into the car park of the Motel in Sedona and came to a halt.

Looking through the window of the bus at the sweeping frontage of the Motel, with its potted palm and ferns all tastefully illuminated – I could see that this would be an expensive place to stay. Remembering Joy's words about the "Motel down the road" – I hoped that Sedona had some cheaper B &Bs if I needed one!

As I retrieved my luggage from the rear of the bus, I saw Joy and Sandra walking towards me - they had huge smiles on their faces.

It was great to meet them at last and we all hugged one another.

The drive to their house only took 10 or fifteen minutes and I soon found myself sitting in their living room with a very welcome cup of tea and - as Joy herself smoked – a cigarette.

I felt right at home.

They gave me the telephone so that I could ring John to let him know that I had arrived and this time, as I finished dialling the number, I heard the phone ringing.

When John answered the telephone, I excitedly blurted out, "Hi – I'm sitting on Joy and Sandra's sofa – it's 9 o' clock, what time is it there?

I was surprised that it was now 4am on Tuesday 26th - back in England.

I had travelled thousands of miles – it had taken 23 hrs and it was still Monday! Would I ever get used to these time zones?

But it was great to speak to him and I know he was relieved to know that I had arrived safely.

Between us, John and I arranged a time every morning, when he would ring me. At the end of my stay – our phone bill was enormous!

Joy showed me into the room that I would be sleeping in. It was a lovely room, which Joy used as her healing room. Leaving – she said, "I'll leave you to unpack – come through into the living room when you're ready."

The first thing I did was to pull Yorrick out of the rucksack.
Placing him on the bed I sat down beside him and looked around me.
"Well – here we are Yorrick – we've arrived."
Still sitting on the bed – but with my feet flat on the floor – I grounded myself and I thanked Wolf, Silver Cloud – and all those people who had brought me safely to Sedona.
Feeling wide-awake – I rejoined Joy and Sandra in the living room, where we spent the rest of the evening chatting and laughing. We also agreed that I would spend two days of my visit having a working session with both of them.

Tuesday 26th May.

On my first night in Sedona I slept for just 4hrs.
At 6am, I woke feeling very refreshed and ready for the day.
Having got washed and dressed – I walked through into the living room.
The sight that befell me was wonderful and unexpected.

Through the large picture windows I could see the huge red rocks of Sedona – just as I had seen on my travels with Silver Cloud. The red rocks were all around – everywhere I looked – and not only one shade of red.

Contained within the red I could see a myriad of different hues, red, oranges, yellows – all of which changed colour as the light changed. And each huge rock was a different shape - bathed in the early morning sunshine – with a backdrop of the bluest sky I had ever physically seen.

I was spellbound.

Remembering the journey in the shuttle bus through the darkness last night – I thanked Silver Cloud for saving this wonderful surprise for me. I felt as though I had woken in a different world. A world full of wonder.

Over breakfast, Joy and Sandra told me that we would be "hitting the streets" at 8.30am – to avoid the heat of the day. They didn't tell me where we were going but still in awe of those red rocks – and more than happy to be guided by them - I was happy to "go with the flow."

Also – having met Joy and Sandra for the first time – I was very aware that they were both strong characters. Both have - sometimes – a wicked sense of humour. Both are very confident and outgoing. And underlying their love and generosity – both are very strong willed.

Joy handed me a full water bottle, which I stuffed into my rucksack, along with Yorrick, my two cameras plus extra film, money, passport, tissues, sun hat and anything else I thought I might need. Clad in the factor 30 and with my sunglasses hanging from a cord around my neck - we set off in the car. And of course - I had my Arizona shoes on my feet.

This was my first real view of Sedona.

The vibrancy of the colours was exactly as I had seen on my travels with Silver Cloud and that vibrancy was energising Everywhere I looked, the contrast of red rock, red desert, cacti and cloudless blue sky was a wonder to behold.

Joy drove at the now familiar sedate pace – pulling off the road by the strangest looking rock I had ever seen.
"This rock is called Bell Rock", she informed me.
Joy and I got out of the car and walked towards the towering Bell Rock.
"What do you feel about this rock?" she asked.
"It feels like a portal – an alien portal" I replied.
"There have been many sightings of Alien spacecraft around here – maybe you'll see one" she mused.
Looking down at my feet to avoid her gaze - my thoughts went to Peter, "Maybe", I muttered. "maybe I will."
Changing the tone of my voice I looked at her and said;
"Hey! – I've just realised - my shoes are the same colour of the sand and rocks – isn't that brilliant!"

Back in the car Joy and Sandra pointed out other rocks to me and told me their names - Courthouse, Cathedral and Chapel Rock.
Looking at the structures I could see where their names had come from – as they did indeed, resemble the buildings they were named after – both in shape and size.

We continued driving down the seemingly straight road with desert and cactus on either side of us.
Our destination was a town called Oak Creek Village.

The town came into view like an oasis in the desert.

Oak Creek Village had several shops – all situated around a large parking area.

"Where do you want to visit first?" asked Sandra.

"Oh – is there a shop that sells luggage?"

Sandra, without hesitation, pointed to a shop on the other side of the car park.

I must explain:

The lady in the Travel Agent had told me that I would be allowed to travel with two bags, plus my hand luggage. She advised me that - if I flew out with one – I could either take an empty bag with me, or buy one when I was in America. That way – I would have a bag to carry any purchases I made during my trip.

This, I thought, was a brilliant idea, and I had decided to buy a bag in Arizona as a momento.

The shop had travel bags of all shapes and sizes and after a few minutes I decided on a red holdall – having calculated the cost on a currency converter – courtesy of my sister in law - I walked over to the cash desk.

"I love your accent" the assistant said – "Are you from England?"

I had a lovely conversation with the assistant, telling her where I lived and proudly announced that this was my first trip abroad. Then, conscious that Joy and Sandra were waiting outside, I excused myself and went to join them.

The sun was really hot by now and I was thankful for the water bottle that Joy had given me.

We walked around a few more shops and I was fascinated by everything that I saw. Even though many goods were familiar to me – I strangely felt as though I was seeing them for the first time.

(During one excursion I visited the giant Wallmart supermarket, where I felt like a child in a toy shop – marvelling at the array of different goods all under the same roof).

Having explored the many different shops, we got into the car and set off retracing our journey through the desert on our return to Sedona.

During the journey, Joy and Sandra asked me questions about my life in Wales? – What food did I like to eat? – and – "How had things settled down, after the bankruptcy?"

One question in particular that I found difficult to answer was from Joy – she asked, "What do you do for fun?"

"Well" I replied – "I listen to music and take the dogs for a walk."

"Yeah" she retorted – "But what do you do for fun?"

I couldn't think of an answer.

That - I found - was a very sobering thought and left me asking myself the same question.

Joy turned off the main road drove down a dusty road that climbed upwards. The car bounced along as we climbed and we arrived at the Chapel of the Holy Cross.

I had never seen anything like this chapel – whose large window protruded from the rock - looking as though is had grown out of the rocks themselves.

Joy explained that the idea for this amazing building was conceived by Marguerite Brunswig.

The chapel, which was completed in 1956, is non-denominational.

Marguerites' desire, was that the Chapel would be for ALL people.

There were many visitors around the Chapel so Joy and Sandra told me that they would wait for me outside while I went in to explore.

The cool quiet interior, when contrasted with the heat and bustle of other visitors outside was overwhelming. The peaceful and solemn energy inside was incredible – almost tangible, and reduced me to tears.

I sat down on one of the pews and listened to the silence.

Some people were lighting candles at the front of the chapel and I decided to join them.

Walking down to the front of the chapel I paid for two candles, lit them and returned to the pew and sat down again.

I felt such a sense of peace in that small chapel and judging by the reaction of other visitors – I knew that I was not alone in that feeling.

Although it is now 10 years later – I feel in my heart – that both those candles still burn brightly.

Emerging from the Chapel and accompanying gift shop, I wandered around – taking lots of photographs.

From this elevated location the views were absolutely tremendous – the weather perfect. I felt that Wolf and Silver Cloud were very close by and thanked them for bringing me to this place.

Driving back into Sedona, Joy and Sandra suggested that I walked around the shops while they attended to some business of their own.

I felt very relaxed as I walked around the town and made one or two small purchases. Everyone was very friendly and – just like on the movies - the words "You're welcome" and "Have a nice day" were much in use. It was wonderful.

The afternoon and evening were spent back at the house relaxing and chatting.

Joy and Sandra have a large welcoming patio which overlooks their garden. Over the next few days – I would spend a lot of time sitting in the shade, gazing at the rocks and watching thin fluffy clouds drifting by.

It was whilst sitting on the patio that I first encountered a Humming Bird. The first thing I noticed was a buzzing noise, which I thought, was a Bee. Looking towards the sound, I saw a humming bird, drinking nectar from a feeder on the patio. It was a most unexpected but wonderful encounter.

That night, as I lay in bed I was suddenly aware that our dog Jill had "travelled" from her bed and was standing beside mine.

"Hello Jill – what are you doing here? Are you OK?" I asked.

She seemed happy to have located me and I said; "Now you've found me you'd better go home – go home to John." "Dusty and Toby (Joy and Sandra's cats) will come and find you – go back to your "dad."

With that, Jill left.

That was Jill's only visit.

Wednesday 27th May.

The day dawned bright and sunny.
I realised that I had slept for only four and a half hours
– yet still I woke feeling refreshed.
I thanked my team for helping me to adapt to the time
changes and I felt sure they understood my wish to be
as active as I could be during my stay.

John rang as usual and I told him about Jill's visit.
"I wondered if that was what she was doing" he replied.
John then explained that at about 5 or 5.15am she had
left her own bed, which was in our bedroom. As she
hadn't returned to the bedroom, John went to look for
her – and found her asleep on my chair in the living
room.

After a relaxed breakfast, Joy and I "hit the streets"
once more and I had the opportunity to visit the local
supermarket.
One thing that struck me whilst looking around the
supermarket– is the size of everything. Melons are huge
– bigger than footballs. And the steaks are of dinner
plate proportions. My walk around the supermarket was
an education in itself. And when Joy told me that she
had to visit the Bank – I was surprised to find that it
was a drive-in bank.
I felt like a child in wonderland.

We drove around the streets where I noticed, to my
delight – those traffic lights I had only seen on films –
the ones that are very high off the ground and are
suspended on cables, which stretch out across the road.
And of course – the very large, often brightly coloured,
cars were all driving on the "wrong" side of the road!

Everywhere I looked – I took a photograph – wanting to record everything I saw so that I could share it with John. Everywhere I looked – the giant red rocks remained the backdrop to each picture.

Joy and I finished our excursion by calling in at drive-in take away to buy our lunch.
I was living the Sedona way – and I loved it.

Joy and Sandra had bought tickets for the cinema in Oak Creek – for that afternoon. So once again, we drove to Oak Creek and I had another chance to see Bell, Courthouse, Cathedral and Church rock.
During that drive, Sandra asked, "Do you want to see snow?"
"Snow!" I repeated, taking a yet another drink from my water bottle.
I looked out of the window as the sun blazed down onto the ground and being wary of Sandra's' wicked sense of humour I added: "What do you mean – snow?"
"Just answer the question." came the reply from the rear seat.
The silence in the car was deafening – as Sandra waited for my answer.

" Yes - that would be great" I replied.
"Good" she said.
 The snow was never mentioned again.

The film that we saw, was an Eagles-eye view over Sedona and the surrounding land.
It was brilliantly filmed and at some points, made my stomach lurch as the camera swooped over the tops of the rocks and hills. I really felt as though I was flying like a bird over the desert far below, daring to swoop perilously close to the giant craggy rocks. The views

stretched for miles and the true of size and enormity of the rocks, which had once – thousands of years ago – been under the sea – revealed itself.

When the film had finished, I was really pleased to be able to buy it in video form. "John will love this" I thought and I think Yorrick enjoyed it too!

During the drive back to Sedona, we stopped at a small grocery shop. Sandra and I went inside and Sandra suggested that I bought a Lottery ticket. "Wouldn't it be great", I thought – "to return home having won the lottery!" John and I have always done the British lottery – so I eagerly bought a ticket.

When I looked at the random numbers that the machine had chosen for me – I was amazed to find that the printed numbers corresponded to certain ages of mine – that held a significance for me.

(Unfortunately – my numbers didn't win me the lottery prize – but I still keep that ticket in my purse all the same).

That evening I saw a shooting star. It was a perfect end to a wonderful day.

Thursday 28th May.

Today had been designated a healing day.

I was to work with both Joy and Sandra – culminating in a couch healing session from Sandra. A healing session which took me so deep into myself, that after it was completed – I had no option but to lie down for half an hour – unable to move.

The workday was to begin at 10am and as I was yet again – up bright and early – I went for a walk around

an area called Schnebly taking my camera and Yorrick
with me.

It was only 8.30 in the morning but the sun was already
very hot. And heeding Joys' warning to take water with
me – I began to drink from the bottle about a minute
into my walk.

Returning to the house with yet another completed roll
of film – I prepared for the day ahead by going to my
room and listening to some of the music that I had
brought with me.

That evening, as darkness fell, we all went to eat at the
Red Planet diner.

The décor had an alien theme, which provided another
photo opportunity.

As I wandered around the diner taking photographs, I
wondered if any of the local diners ever played that
game we play in Wales – Spot the Tourist!

I was given the choice of either, sitting at a table – or at
the counter. I chose the counter as I thought that was
the American way - and we ordered the food from the
comprehensive menu.

Suddenly a very large dish of salad was placed before
me, a dish that I hadn't ordered. Joy explained that this
was my starter salad. She told me that this is quite
normal – you eat as much as you want – and then you
can take the rest home.

I'd heard of the phrase "Doggy" bag – but never
"Bunny" bag!

To be polite – I picked at the salad – barely making any
dent on the pile – and although I hate wasting food – I
did decline their kind offer to put it in a bag.

After the meal, there was just time to take a picture of me sitting on the wall with the diner in the background before we drove up onto Airport Road in Sedona.

From its high vantagepoint we sat in the car looking out over the town - deep in the silence of our own thoughts. Down below us were the twinkling lights of the houses - above us in the night sky – clouds were slowly drifting by.

I saw another shooting star, which was – yet again - a perfect end to a brilliant day.

When we got home I told Joy and Sandra that I would go to my room.

I felt that they would both enjoy some free time – and I could spend time writing in my notebook, listening to my music and hopefully – speak to Silver Cloud.

This was a pattern that suited us all – and one that we naturally followed every evening.

That evening as I headed towards my room, Sandra called out:

"Be ready to hit the streets at 8am – you and I are going on a journey."

Friday 29th May.

Promptly at 8am, Sandra and I set off on our journey.

Easing even more, into my newfound, "going with the flow" attitude, I didn't ask where our journey was taking us – I was just happy to be going.

Placing my rucksack containing cameras and film – Yorrick – water bottle – money and anything else I thought I might need – into the well of the car floor – I squeezed my feet into the car, sat down and eagerly anticipated the journey.

We stopped at a place called Oak Creek Canyon.
There, I was able to meet a group of Navaho Indians, who sold their wares to the passing motorists.
It was a wonderful experience and I selected a pottery bear for me, and bowl for John as momentoes of that meeting.
Getting back into the car – the road began to creep ever upward through dense forests of pine trees. The trees were amazing – standing straight, and reaching towards the blue sky.
At one point along the road, Sandra stopped the car, explaining that she was just going to get some water.
Puzzled – I too got out of the car. Sandra opened the boot and brought out two plastic water containers. It was then that I noticed a tap on the end of a long pipe – just on the roadside. Sandra, whilst filling a bottle from the tap, explained that the water was mountain water and was very good for drinking, being very pure.
Having filled the water bottles, we got back in the car and continued on our way.

As we climbed higher, I began to feel dizzy. Mentioning this to Sandra, she told me that we would eventually climb to 8,ooo ft above sea level – our destination was to be Flagstaff.

"Keep drinking water", she advised "It'll help."
Periodically sipping water from my bottle – the headache disappeared.

I was really excited.
Flagstaff was one of those places I had heard of.
It sounded such a "romantic" - "American", place to visit. I could hardly wait.

As we drove towards the town, and as the buildings came into view – I was in an instant, no longer sitting in the car – but I was sitting atop a horse drawn wagon. I was dressed in a long grey frock over which I wore a long white pinafore. My head – shielded from the sun by a large white bonnet.

"Where have you gone?" Sandra asked.
Looking at her, I replied, "I feel as though I've travelled this road before – but on a wagon. The land seems familiar"
"That wouldn't surprise me" she replied.
The moment passed and we drove on.

Our first stop, as we entered Flagstaff, was at a drive-in Diner. It was the type of Diner, where you park up by a little intercom and order your food and then someone delivers it to you on a tray, which fixes onto the car window.
Very clever and very convenient.
Again – this was something that I had seen on the television – and here I was experiencing it - Great!

After we had eaten, Sandra said that she would drive around Flagstaff so that I could see the sights.
As we drove down the road we both noticed, to my delight and amusement – a large convertible car in front of us. In the rear seat of the car, sat a large woolly, St Bernard type dog.
The dog – like the driver - was wearing a sun visor. The dog also wore a look of supremacy on its face, as it looked about – surveying its' surroundings.

The next sight that came into view was extraordinary.
Looking into the distance I saw a snow topped mountain.

"Snow" I exclaimed.

Sandra laughed – "I did ask you if you wanted to see snow."

It was hard to contemplate that there could be snow on such a hot day. It was a very picturesque sight – but sadly – too far away for my small camera.

As we continued to drive around I could hear the clanking of bells. I recognised this noise from television and films that I had watched. It was the sound of the trains as they chugged into the station.

Flagstaff is well known for it's clanging trains, and shortly after I had returned from Arizona, I met someone who had stayed overnight in Flagstaff, and he hadn't been able to sleep for the clanging of the bells.

To me, on this brief visit – they were music to my ears.

Driving past the station I was thrilled to see the snow topped mountain return into view, and this time, I did manage to take a couple of photographs.

Before we headed back onto the road out of Flagstaff, Sandra stopped at a supermarket. This was a brilliant opportunity for me to buy a birthday card for each of them – as during one evenings conversation they had told me that their birthdays were on the 1st and 3rd of June. I had already chosen a stone for each of them – out of the collection that I had brought with me. And would look for another gift as I visited different places.

Leaving Flagstaff, Sandra took a detour around an outlying residential area.

All the houses were on large plot of land, and nestled amongst tall pine trees. Parked in most driveways – were three vehicles. Everybody seemed to own a camper van, a utility vehicle and a large car – and as this was early on a Friday afternoon – I surmised that there would be at least one other vehicle, who's owner was still at work.

They do love their cars in America.

Continuing our journey on a forest road – Sandra turned off the main road and drove into the forest itself. She parked the car and said, "You go and have a walk around. – I'll wait for you here."

Leaving the car, I walked into the forest and sat under the shade of a pine tree. Silver Cloud and Wolf joined me and we spent some precious time talking together.

I thanked them for bringing me to Arizona and thanked them for being with me.

They sat beside me and - in peaceful familiarity – we listened to the sounds of the forest.

After a short space of time Silver Cloud said, *"Time to go."*

Standing up to return to the car, I spied three stones lying together on the ground nearby – I picked them up saying – "These will always remind me of this place and this time spent with you."

Near to the stones, was a piece of wood that I had noticed earlier. I noticed it because the shape of the wood resembled a Beaver.

I walked over to the "beaver", picked him up, and placed him under the tree. "There you are little beaver – sit in the shade."

Walking away from the tree – I turned my head – the little beaver was still sitting there – fast asleep.

Silver Cloud and Wolf had gone.

Climbing back into the car, Sandra headed off back to the main road. As we joined the main road, there in front of us was another "icon" of Americanism – a bright yellow school bus.

Apparently – in America – it is illegal to overtake a school bus – so obeying that law – we crawled along behind it.
I'm glad I saw this icon – but a further 2 miles down the road – I was relieved when it turned right, and disappeared from view.

Travelling back towards Sedona through the pine forests I had time to reflect on my stay, thus far.
Each day had been a journey of discovery.
It was blatantly obvious to me that, Joy and Sandra were working hard. Every conversation, every place we visited, was for a purpose. I knew that they were following instructions from their Guides. They were being led – as I was being led and I was happy to follow.
As if to interrupt my thoughts, Sandra suddenly pulled off the road and parked the car.
"Go and look at the river at the bottom of the bank" she suggested.
I looked in the direction of Sandra's pointing finger – and opened the car door.
Slithering down the bank, I arrived at a pool of water.
Edging the pool, were grey boulders of various sizes.
Not being a spontaneous person – I surprised myself by taking my shoes and socks off. I just had to step into the water.
It was freezing!
Sandra, who had stayed near to the car, shouted:
"You know that snow you saw – well this water comes down from that mountain."

My feet were now beginning to feel really cold – so I came out of the water and sat on a hot, comfortable rock The sun filtered down through the trees onto my wet cold feet and began to dry them. This reminded me of that time when Silver Cloud and I had been joined by Buffalo and Armon. The time when the sun had dried the sand off my legs – and the time when the pine cone had released its seeds.

The *"seeds of new beginnings."*

Jolted back from that memory, I quickly realised that I was not alone.

In the bushes across the other side of the pool there was an energy. An energy that I didn't recognise – but an energy that I knew, came with love.

The energy began to emerge from the bushes that led far back into the forest. And he – I knew it was a male energy – came and stood between the rocks that were facing me from across the pool.

The energy spoke to me:

He told me that he was *"energy"*, and not a person.

He told me that he would speak to me at a *"later date."*

Then he faded back into the bushes and beyond.

I heard a noise behind me and turning round – saw that Sandra was coming to join me.

I told her what I had seen and heard and then she asked: "Do you want an ice cream?"

"Yes – that would be great – my treat" I replied as I replaced my shoes and socks."

We began to climb back up to the car – but not before we had each chosen a stone as a momento.

Driving a little further down the road, we reached an area – Oak Creek Canyon - which was a popular stopping place – as it was a great vantage point to view the river down below in the valley.

In the car park there was a small café with a kiosk from which ice creams were sold.

As we were walking towards the kiosk, a voice from behind us called out Sandra's name. Standing still – we turned round and a lady, who was Native American, came up to us.

Sandra introduced me to her and she greeted me by bringing her hands together towards her face – and bowing her head.

The greeting that I had seen and used myself – when travelling with Silver Cloud.

The lady emitted a calm peace – which shone in her face and eyes and for a split second I was transfixed.

I didn't know whether to reply in the same manner – and then - the moment was gone.

After a short conversation with Sandra, she said her goodbyes, adding, " I will leave you to your day."

Sandra and I walked over to the kiosk to buy the ice creams. I had asked for a small ice cream – but was now holding the biggest "small" ice cream I had ever set my eyes on.

Sandra turned to me, and asked, "Do you know what that greeting means?" referring to her friend.

"No" I replied "I use it, but only when I'm with Spirit."

"It means" she explained – "I respect your Soul."

I wished that I had been quick enough and brave enough, to return her greeting.

Back on the road, we visited Bell rock again and I collected a tiny amount of desert and put it in an empty film canister.

I was still amazed by the vibrant colours of my surroundings and I was determined to show John a sample of the red sand – not merely a photograph.

By this time – the heat was beginning to make me wilt and, having taken yet more photographs – I was relieved to sit back in the car.

Driving into Sedona, Sandra asked me if I wanted to visit any shops.

I wanted to buy a present for Jack and Jill, and having seen the decorative wind sock that hung over their patio I replied that I would like to buy something similar to take home with me.

Sandra can be a woman of few words sometimes.

In silence, she made a couple of turns down roads I had not driven down before and parked the car in front of – what I can only describe as a - windsock shop!

This building was bedecked with colourful windsocks in all shapes and sizes. The interior of the shop was similarly decorated. Huge multicoloured kites hung from the ceiling – and in every direction that I looked – there was different kites and socks, some in the shape of animals.

The shop stood out in its surroundings like an oasis.

I bought my windsock and a few presents for people back home, and then having visited a pet shop and bought two squeaky green frogs.

We returned home.

As the sun set that evening, the sky went pink – pink for as far as the eye could see.

We all went and stood at the front of the house – me with my camera of course.

As I looked through the viewfinder, I clearly saw an angel in the sky. Removing my eye from the lens, I looked again into the sky and the angel had disappeared.

Holding the camera to my eye once more – I saw the angel again.

I explained this phonomenum to Joy, who looked and witnessed the same thing. Handing the camera back to me, she said, "Take a picture, and ask the angels to show themselves."

I took several photographs and when they were developed – I was pleased and grateful, to see one pink angel.

Later, just before I went to my room, Joy gave me a gift of a pendant. The pendant was a silver angel and in the middle of it – there was a tiny Yin Yang symbol.

Thanking her – I immediately placed it on one of the chains that I wore round my neck.

This had been a truly remarkable day and as I went to sleep that night, the energy that I had met at the pool, stood by my bed and watched over me.

Saturday 30th May.

I woke early again this morning - feeling very emotional and light headed. I was aware of the presence of the energy that I had met yesterday.

I grounded myself, washed and dressed, and went out into the kitchen to make a cup of tea.

Still feeling light headed – I returned to my room to listen to some music and to ground myself once more.

As I sat on the edge of the bed, I felt the new energy move away, and the familiar vibration of Wolf move very close to me.

Standing by my side – Wolf spoke in a quiet clear voice. His words astounded me – Wolf told me he was leaving.

There was hardly a moment in which I could react to this devastating news - as he quickly and quietly walked away.

Shocked and upset, I began to cry – calling after him, "Wolf - Wolf – come back so that I can talk to you!"

As I felt him continuing to move further away from me – I shouted, "Thankyou Wolf – thankyou for everything!"

The energy that I had met at the pool the day before, immediately enveloped me – causing me to become light headed and dizzy. I knew I had no alternative other than to ask him to step away.

He didn't step away.

I called for Silver Cloud, and as I did – the new energy bore down on me even more.

Thinking quickly I wondered if this new energy was a new doorkeeper so I tentatively asked him to help me to ground myself.

Gradually, my dizziness began to ease – as I felt the excess energy seep into the floor.

Taking a few minutes more – I repeated my grounding exercise – with – I have to say – some considerable help from the "presence."

Glancing at the clock, I realised that John would be ringing any minute, so I made my way into the living room to receive his call. The phone rang and hearing John's voice - I immediately blurted out that Wolf had left. After a brief conversation, we said goodbye and I went to sit out on the porch to contemplate Wolf's departure – and to ask Silver Cloud "What the new energy was?"

Yet again, it was another sunny day. The red rocks were silhouetted against the blue sky and the humming birds were already feeding from the feeders that Joy and Sandra put out for them.

I heard Silver Cloud calling my name. Relieved, I looked towards a far distant hill where I saw him standing on the very top of it.

He waved but his energy told me that this was not a wave of greeting - but a wave of farewell.

"No!" I called "Don't go!"

Silver Cloud spoke briefly and told me that the time had come when he and I must part.

I was devastated.

The emotion that I had woken with overwhelmed me.

I shouted at him. "No you can't go – you can't leave me here!"

But his silent expression told me otherwise.

Silver Cloud had, over the years, given myself, John and others so much good advice.

He had shared his personal thoughts with us - thus giving of himself.

He had steered me through the good - and not so good times.

He had always guided and encouraged me, even when I had been angry or sulking.

He had taught me to communicate - using simple, uncomplicated - step by step instructions.

He and Wolf had kept me safe.

And they had given me the confidence to open up to a succession of wonderful communicators.

He had been patient, caring, unconditionally loving and often - humorous.

Silver Cloud had brought me to his wonderful land - and – I loved him.

Realising that we had little time left and that his leaving was imminent and definite - I hurriedly thanked him for everything that he had taught me.

I thanked him for bringing me to this place.

I told him that I loved him – and would always love him.

And finally – I cried – "What will I do without you!"

My feeble words could not express my gratitude and the love that I had for him.

By now, I was sobbing.

I sobbed until I could cry no more.

Drying my eyes – I looked towards the hill.

The hill was empty - and so was I.

Outside Chicago Airport

Bell Rock on the left

Courthouse Rock on the left

Oak Creek Village

Chapel of the Holy Cross
Sedona

Joy (left) Me and Sandra

A view across Sedona, taken from the Chapel

Traffic lights in Sedona

A house near to Joy and Sandra's

West Sedona

Outside the Red Planet Diner

Sandra collecting water

Snow in Flagstaff

A residential area on the ouskirts of Flagstaff

A beautiful wood on the ouskirts of Flagstaff

"Littler Beaver"

Me by an "icy" pool

"Steamboat"

The view of the distant hill as seen from the Patio

Spirits Fly High

CHAPTER THREE

BLUE SKIES OVER SEDONA

Saturday 30th May *(continued)*

When I went back into the house, Joy, who had seen and heard me crying, asked me what had happened. I told her that both Wolf and Silver Cloud had left and that I felt lost.
"We've been together for three and a half years" I wailed.

Joy listened sympathetically, and then said, "Well – go and get ready – we're hitting the streets in half an hour – and then this afternoon, we've got tickets for the circus."

A couple of days ago, Joy and Sandra had asked me if I wanted to go to see a circus, and the expression on my face must have given away my reluctance.
"Don't you like the circus?" they asked.

Actually, I had only ever been to one circus as a child, and I didn't like performing animals. Neither did I enjoy watching the high wire acts that I had seen on television. My stomach would churn and my hands would sweat, as the artists swung back and fro.

"Are there any animals?" I asked.

"No!" – Joy exclaimed, "Definitely no animals."

"Would you like to go?"

"Yes" I replied "That sounds good", I still wasn't sure?

I went to my room and gathered my things together and having filled my water bottle I waited quietly in the hall for Joy and Sandra.

Setting off in the car – I sat looking out of the window as the desert and red rocks passed by.
My thoughts were with Wolf and Silver Cloud. I was remembering some of the things that they had said - remembering some of the things that they had shown me - and wishing that the three of us were sitting on that tiny beach, by the river – wishing that everything was normal.
Still deep in thought, I realised that we had pulled off the main road and were driving down a narrower, dusty one. Joy parked the car, and we stepped out under a very hot sun.

I felt as though I was standing in a small wilderness. There was no car park – just land. And all around – there were bushes and trees.

"This is Red Rock Crossing" Joy announced, "We thought you would like it here – go and wander about – try down there first."
Joy was pointing to a small path, which led between the trees. I followed her direction and walked along the sandy path.

As I walked through the trees, I heard the sound of rippling water and headed towards the direction of the sound.

I arrived at a tiny beach by a river - it was all so familiar to me - I was staggered.

I realised that this was – "our" beach – Silver Clouds' Wolf's and mine.

With tears falling down my face, I sat down.

"Silver Cloud – where are you – I'm here at our place, Silver Cloud!" – I called.

I looked towards the path to my right – a path that I knew well.

Watching, waiting, listening and expecting Wolf to come for me, as he had done in the past.

But today, there was just an empty path.

The sadness of the morning's events overwhelmed me – made more unbearable because – here I was - sitting on this tiny beach – alone.

After all the visits I had made to this place on my travels – to be sitting here, a short time after Wolf and Silver Cloud had left – increased the pain that their leaving had created.

Tears silently fell down my face and the pain in my heart increased.

The energy that had been with me all night was gone – and I was left alone with my pain and memories.

Suddenly – the pain began to ease.

Wiping the tears away from my face, I laughed out loud.

"Silver Cloud – this is just like you – I suppose you think this is funny?"

Recalling Silver Clouds wry sense of humour and holding his love inside me – I realised - that my being in this very spot – on this very morning – was a great gift.

A final gift from Silver Cloud.

Gratitude flooded through my body – flushing my pain away.

"Oh – Thankyou Silver Cloud – Thankyou Wolf. Thankyou for bringing me to this place."

Looking around me, I saw two leaves lying on the ground.
Picking them up - I placed the two leaves - one for Silver Cloud and one for Wolf – into the river.
I watched as the leaves surfed the tiny waves - and disappeared from view.

"Bye Silver Cloud – Bye Wolf" - I called.
"Thankyou!"

Looking across the river I saw the familiar "island" that I had seen many times before.

Often I had asked Silver Cloud, "What is on the other side of the island?" and he would only reply with a smile.
Today, I asked the same question and today I received the answer:
Me – I am on the other side of the island.
The big wide world in on the other side of the island - and now I am here.
Not sadly, with Wolf and Silver Cloud by my side – but – forever in my heart.

I thanked Silver Cloud for his teachings and for guiding me on my journey.
I thanked Wolf for all the protection he had given to me and others.
I ending my homily - "I love you Silver Cloud."
"I love you Wolf."

Knowing that the time was right for me to move on, I stood up, and as I did – I saw three stones lying in a circle together, on the ground. Picking the three stones up I placed them in my rucksack. Taking my camera – I took photographs of the river – the beach – and the pathway and with one last look about me – I set off to rejoin Joy and Sandra.

Finding Joy and Sandra sitting on the ground, patiently waiting for me, I excitedly told them how I had been to this place before.
I told them about the travels that I had had with Wolf and Silver Cloud.
I told them how the three of us had often sat down by the river – described the path that Wolf would walk down - and told them the island story.
I thanked Joy and Sandra for bringing me here today.
And silently – I thanked their Guides for the very important part that they were playing – to facilitate this wonderful journey of mine.

With my spirits lifting by the minute – we took some photographs of each other during which there was a lot of laughing. Then, at their suggestion – I went to explore in another direction.

This short walk led me to what I feel - is the most wonderful spot on the whole planet.
A place where the clear sparkling river widens and rushes over rocks, creating eddies and pools that sparkle in the sunlight. And the backdrop to this brilliant place – and towering into the sky – is the most tremendous view of Cathedral Rock.

I took loads of photographs, wishing to record every aspect of the scene - and then – having explored every

avenue through my camera lens – I sat down on a warm
rock at the rivers' edge. Taking Yorrick out of the
rucksack – he and I sat in silence - listening to the
sound of the babbling river and the birdsong. As I sat
gazing at Cathedral rock I began to soak in the tranquil,
majestic energy that it exuded. I marvelled at the
wonders of the Universe – and at the marvels' of the
Spirit world who, had combined their efforts with Joy
and Sandra – and had brought me to this very special
place.

All too soon - it was time for us to leave.
Reluctantly - I climbed back into the car – glancing
once more, before I did, at that amazing view of
Cathedral Rock against the eternal blue sky.

The circus was in a town called Cottenwood.
Driving through the desert land I gazed out of the car
windows taking in the views.
I still thrilled at the sight of cactus!
And the sight of the shimmering red land, huge red
rocks – and the eternal blue sky - remains emblazoned
on my brain forever.
In fact – on my return home – and whenever I spy a
small patch of blue sky peeking through an otherwise
grey day – I look at it and say to myself – "Stick it on
your brain."
Sometimes – in the UK – blue sky can be a rare
commodity and I don't like to waste the opportunity
whenever I see it.

I think that it was on this day that I ate my first Taco.

Unfortunately my note taking fails to record the exact day of this momentous event! However, I do remember eating and enjoying a mincemeat filled Taco – my first ever "exotic" meal!

Like other towns that I had seen on my travels around Sedona – the town of Cottonwood suddenly came into view – nestling in the desert like an oasis.

We arrived at the circus with about ½ hr to spare.
A ½ hr during which we queued in line in the open air.
I can't stress how hot it was on this early afternoon.
Now I understood why Joy and Sandra took me out in the mornings – which themselves were hot.
As always - I was smothered in Factor 30 – wore clothes with long sleeves and never stepped outside without my hat and sunglasses.
But even my continuous gulps of water from my water bottle – did not reduce my rising temperature.

Feeling very "English" and a little feeble - my only consolation was that everyone else was beginning to wilt under the heat and when the announcement came – that the "tent was open" – there was a mad dash to dive into the relative cool of the tent.
I say relative, because the initial feeling I got on entering the tent was that the temperature was indeed a lot lower – this feeling was not to last.

I followed Joy and Sandra into the tent and up the tiered steps to the very top of the rows of seats.
To my delight – the rear of the tent was open – allowing a warm (if not cool) breeze, to blow on our backs.

The circus was absolutely incredible!

I can only describe the acts as "choreographed dances in the air."

All the acts were performed on high wires and ropes which were tethered to the ground. The many different costumes were intricate, theatrical and colourful. And the music and lighting created a magical energy.
Both adults and children performed in the circus and I sat enthralled and amazed.
The temperature in the tent was rising and I spotted a man selling drinks. Feeling dehydrated – I chose the biggest Coca-Cola drink I could buy – and those of you who have been to America yourselves, will know that "big" means "humungous" in American speak.

It was a truly amazing spectacle and I was so grateful to Joy and Sandra for giving me the opportunity to experience this excellent show.

We left the circus before the show had finished as Joy had a sitting with two people that evening. Although I had been enthralled by the show – I was glad to escape the sweltering heat of the circus tent. I could only marvel (again) at the fitness and stamina of the performers both adults and children.

That evening Joy had a sitting with a client but she had invited me to join them all later on for a channelling session.
So just before the client and his girlfriend arrived, I retired to my room.
I spent the evening sitting cross-legged on the floor, listening to music and "raising my vibrations" – taking copious sips of Cola in order to quench my still persistent thirst.

(OK – I know it should have been water – but the caffeine in the Cola replaced the caffeine my body was missing after my tea bags had run out!)

The energy that had been with me that morning was still present – still persistent, and when I asked – "Who are you?" he replied – *"I am wind – I am rock - I am anything I want to be."*

At around 9.15pm, Sandra knocked on my door and asked me to come to join them for the channelling session.

Preparing for this – I asked the new energy to let me know if there was anything Spirit wanted me to do during the session.

After the introductions were made, we all took our places on the chairs on the patio and Joy began the channelling.

As the channelling became higher and Joy went deeper into it, both Sandra and I simultaneously lifted our arms to assist in the holding of the energy field.

It was a wonderful session and I was grateful to Joy for inviting me to join in.

Sunday 31st June.

The man who had had a sitting with Joy, the evening before – was a ranger and guide. His name was Dave – and he, along with his girlfriend Pat - had agreed to take us up into the mountains to visit a cave.

The walk, I was told, would be about 2½ miles.

Setting off at 8.30am that Sunday morning - I was very excited at the prospect of this trek. I was also thankful to Silver Cloud – who - a few weeks before, had encouraged me to update my Tetanus injection.

We all climbed into Dave's big all-terrain-vehicle and he drove us to a place called Secret Canyon - a vast area of mountainous terrain. As soon as I got out of the car, I could feel that Secret Canyon was definitely more imposing in nature than all those fantastic giant red rocks with their friendly names – Coffee pot – Steamboat – Bell – Cathedral and Courthouse.

We waited as Dave began to clad himself in protective leg-ware, which he explained, would guard against snake-bites. On hearing this, and noticing that Pat was wearing sturdy walking boots - I had one moment of hesitation as I looked down at my training shoes. Seeing that Joy and Sandra were similarly attired - I dismissed any doubts that I had.

Dave signed a visitor's book, which was fastened to a wooden plinth – filling in the details of the time we set off and the number in the party.
The signing in – and out – of this book is a necessity. People have become lost in this land and unfortunately, I was told – only a few weeks ago, a man had entered the canyon and had never returned.
All attempts to find him had ended in failure.
So it was with this in mind and with our water bottles to hand - that we set off in single file behind our guide – who now carried a staff.

Walking slowly in single file allowed for time to examine at close range, the variety of native plants.
As we climbed higher, the views - through the many small trees and bushes - of the surrounding hills was awesome.
At one point along the path – the trees opened up providing a view of the distant red hills - and of course – the constant blue sky.

Extending out from the top of a hill I saw a trail of cloud reaching upwards into the sky.

For me – the trail resembled a smoke signal as used by Indians to relay a message. Reaching for my camera, I stopped to take a photograph.

As I did – I knew that Silver Cloud was watching. His message was - that although he and I were no longer working together, we would always be connected.

I knew that whatever I did – and who ever else I worked with – Silver Cloud and his teachings – would remain with me forever.

With renewed vigour I continued onward and upward.

It was hot and the climb was steady and relentless - the air was becoming thinner.

I had to stop many times to catch my breath and drink from my water bottle – but each stop gave another opportunity to wonder at the ever changing view.

We heard a wolf baying in the distance – it's call – answered by another – I felt as though I was in a truly magical – yet hazardous world.

This was my only encounter with the wildlife that inhabited this land – unless you count the evening that Joy drew my attention to the wild Boar that were on their nocturnal ritual of snuffling through the garden.

Our trek eventually led us to a cave, the entrance of which remained hidden from view until the very last minute.

The cave was brilliant. Quite large and cool and set deep into the rock - it was a welcome respite from the heat, but the most incredible aspect to the cave – were the handprints and drawings around the walls.

It was amazing to think of those ancient people who had lived here and who had decorated their space with these incredible drawings.

I couldn't resist placing my own hands into some of the handprints.
There was one area of the cave – which I felt was a more sacred area than the rest of it. A patch of sandy earth, which I walked around – as opposed to walked over. I asked Joy what was special about that place and she told me that that it was a place where the elders would have sat and talked and made plans.

Moving to the middle of the cave, yet within the mouth of the cave itself, I sat down and took my angel pendant off - laying it on a small rock, which was touched by the suns' rays. I asked that the pendant be energised and watched as the angel shimmered in the sunlight.
Looking out in front of me the vista was tremendous. As far as the eye could see there were bushes trees and mountains – the view stretched for miles and miles.
I felt that beyond those far away mountains – the whole wide world was waiting to be explored. Much like the "island" at Red Rock Crossing.
I wondered if one of the artists of the walls had felt like that - and had set off on his or her journey of discovery.

So much had changed within a few short days.
The departure of Wolf and Silver Cloud.
The arrival of this new energy.
I took some minutes to meditate and ask that my own energy remained balanced.

When I had finished I looked down to the floor of the cave – there - lying near my feet, was a small stick which resembled a walking stick. Picking the stick and the angel pendant up, I thanked "them" for their help and acknowledged their gift of the walking aid.

This was to be the first of several walking sticks that have been given to me over the years.

I wandered around the cave, touching the walls and stooping to pick up the sand – opening my fingers to release the sand back onto the floor. I could feel the "new energy" near to me. And as I continued to wander around and absorb the energy of the cave – so he walked alongside me.
Noticing two small stones on the floor, I bent down and picked them up.

"One for each of us" I told him "As a momento of our visit." Sitting down again, looking out onto the far distant horizon – I asked what I should call him - I received no answer.

Conscious that I had taken myself away from the others – and indeed - they had given me the space to be on my own – I rejoined Joy, Sandra, Dave and Pat.

The cave was such a peaceful place and I felt privileged to have been able to visit it.

Keeping an eye on the time of day – and aware of the rising heat – Dave said that we must begin our descent.

The walk back to the car park revealed different spectacular views of the surrounding area – and although the heat and general tiredness tried to hinder my enjoyment – the thrill of it all kept me alert and watchful.

At one point, we all rested for a while and Dave and Pat produced some packets of salted peanuts and shared them around. How grateful was I to eat those nuts!
Such a simple food – but so quick to replace the salts that our bodies had lost.

Feeling refreshed, we continued in single file and eventually stepped out into the open space that was the car park.

Myself, Joy and Sandra thanked Dave and Pat for a wonderful, safe journey – and gratefully climbed into the rear of their car.
Dave drove back to Joy and Sandra's and he and Pat came in for something to eat and drink.
During the conversation, Pat asked if I would be at Joy and Sandra's birthday party which was being held on the coming Saturday.
"No" I replied sadly – "I've got to leave on Thursday."
"Well" – she responded – "if you can change your flights – you can always come and stay with us – we would love to have you stay."

I was astounded at her invitation – I could feel that this was not an empty gesture – and I thanked her very much. Momentarily – the tempting thought crossed my mind that I could possibly stay? I was having such an amazing time and I didn't want it to end.

Yet – John and Jack and Jill were waiting for my return – and the face of the stern customs man at the airport, who knew when I should be leaving, came into my vision.

"Thankyou very much" I repeated – "But I'll go home on Thursday."

Having said goodbye to Dave and Pat, Joy, Sandra and I decided that a rest was in order so we each disappeared to our respective rooms.

It was great to lie down in my cool room and have the time to reflect on the morning's trip.

Without the care of our guide – the trip would not have been possible at all. I would not have missed that particular journey for all the tea in china.

And – to have spent time in that ancient cave was - to say the least – inspiring and humbling.

Late that afternoon, I sat on the patio watching clouds wafting slowly by. As usual I was taking photographs and to my delight, an Angel appeared once more.

As she drifted by – the idea came into my mind that I should have a drum to use in distant healing.

At that exact moment, Joy came to join me. "Do you want to visit the shops – is there something you want to buy?" she asked.

Un-surprised by her ability to "read my mind" and mindful that her Guides had brought her to the patio – I told her that I would like to buy a drum.

"I know just the place, get your things together, we'll go now."

Joy drove me to a shop that sold authentic Native American artefacts.

As soon as I walked into the shop I knew exactly which drum I wanted. It stood out amongst a group of others as if to say "Here I am!"

It was larger than I had anticipated, but I knew that this particular hoop drum was the right drum for me. A selection of drumsticks was shown to me and I spent a few minutes making my choice.

Thanking the assistant, and holding the drum and stick proudly in both hands, Joy and I left the shop.

Joy drove down the road, and parked the car outside a shop that sold anything and everything Angelic.

It never ceased to amaze me, that although I had been taken on several tours in and around Sedona – the myriad of specialist shops was amazing – they seemed to appear out of nowhere!
This particular shop was crammed with statues, ornaments, books, pictures, cards and much, much more. In fact everything Angelic you could imagine!
I had never been in a shop like it.
It was one of those shops that - because there is so much to see – you don't know where to start.
Quickly, I was drawn to a display of small white teddy bears. They were all dressed as Angels.
I selected the one with the cutest face (in my opinion).
"Yorrick" I whispered – "I've found you a little friend."

Yorricks' little friend has a squidgy tummy, and when you press her tummy – she says, in her Girly American accent – "I'm your Guardian Angel."

O.K – My sister wasn't impressed either!
But – she is very cute – the bear I mean - not my sister!

Later that evening we went to a diner for a meal. A simple meal of chicken and chips – or should I say – fries – and after a long physical day – they were very welcome indeed.
Just as we were finishing our meal and simultaneously, we all glanced out of the nearby picture window.
In the car park outside – a car had driven in and parked up. As we watched - a young man in his twenties got

out of the driver's seat and started to walk towards the door of the diner.

The very noticeable thing about this otherwise, normal activity was that – on this balmy evening – the young man was wearing a very long black overcoat - which although open – he held closely to his body.

As he walked across the car park towards the diner entrance, he was looking around him. He looked very furtive indeed.

Joy and Sandra immediately gathered their bags and told me to do the same, "Time to leave" they said.

For the first time on this entire trip – I was unnerved.
"Was a robbery about to take place?" "What was the man concealing under that unseasonable coat?"

Having already paid the bill – we left the diner and the incident was never mentioned again.

I had - up until now – felt totally relaxed and happy during my entire trip. Never once had I felt insecure, fearful or threatened.

This incident intruded into my magical mystery tour – but also served as a timely reminder that complacency can be a dangerous thing.

We never heard of anything bad happening in that diner – thankfully.

Monday 1st June. Joys birthday.

The morning was taken up by celebrating Joy's birthday.

Knowing that Joy and Sandra were expecting visitors I wondered if I should go out – but Joy and Sandra assured me that they wanted me to share in the day.

Friends and family, including the lady who Sandra and I had met in the car park at Oak Creek Canyon - dropped by with gifts for both Joy and Sandra (It would be Sandra's' birthday in two days time). It was a very relaxing, happy and joyous morning and all the visitors made me to feel very welcome.

Joy and Sandra had arranged to go to the Cinema – a traditional birthday treat – and they asked me to join them.

Aware that my holiday was coming to an end, and that tomorrow would be another "working" day for me - I explained that I wanted to spend as much time as I could seeing Sedona – so I declined their offer.

They, in turn, suggested that I went on an organised guided tour. Visitors, they explained, could take a motorised tram tour around all the well-known sites.

It sounded ideal, Yorrick and I would enjoy this – we had never been on a tram before.

After lunch, Joy and Sandra dropped me off in Sedona – right by the tram station. Arranging a time and place to meet later that afternoon, they continued on-to the cinema.

So that sunny afternoon, Yorrick and I joined other tourists on a sight seeing tour of Sedona.

The tour went to some places that I had already visited, but also to places that I had not.

We travelled to the Chapel of the Holy Cross and visited a place called Boynton Canyon. Here – the tram stopped – allowing us passengers to wander around for 15 minutes. Walking around the base of the canyon – our driver and guide pointed up to caves that were visible, high in the rocks. He told us how Native Americans had lived within the caves and I smugly thought to myself – "I bet they're not as special as the cave that I visited."

Back on the road, we passed a Ranch which had horses in a corral - another typical American scene - and on the way back into Sedona, we drove past the Red Planet Diner where we had eaten dinner on Thursday evening.

The tram even swept into the car park of the Motel where I had first arrived – and from which I would depart in two days time – a sobering thought, and one that I preferred not to think about.

All in all – it was a wonderful afternoon and I was grateful that the roof of the tram provided welcome shade from the very hot sun.

The one downside to the trip was the wooden slatted seating covered by a thin foam cushion that slid around underneath you. Ouch! So my advice for anyone who fancies taking the Trolley bus in Sedona is – "take a cushion!"

I was the first to arrive at our meeting place, and whilst waiting for Joy and Sandra – another icon of Americanism - the fire truck – drove past me.

Thankfully the truck didn't seem to be out on an emergency – so I stood happily watching, as it disappeared from view. I was even quick enough to take a photograph of half of it!

Tuesday 2nd June.

Today I worked with Joy and Sandra, resolving some issues surrounding my childhood.

The day's session ended with a second couch healing session with Sandra.

At the end of Thursday's couch healing session I had been unable to move for half an hour. It had taken me all that time to ground myself and return to "normal."

So as this session began, I really didn't know what to expect. Whilst I was lying on the couch, during this healing session with Sandra - she "took" me into a room and asked me if there was anyone else in the room, and if so – who.

Looking into the corner of the room, I saw an angel who told me his name was Gabriel.
Gabriel led me along a pink pathway.
The pathway - I discovered – was a path through the emotional body layer of my aura.
Our walk took us through other layers of my aura and finally – inside my body.
The whole session was amazing.

Sandra ended the session and waited while I "returned" to my body.

Sandra and I then went to into the living room, where Joy was waiting for us.
As I sat on the sofa, Joy handed me a medallion. Engraved on the medallion was a portrait of an angel - and the name inscribed around it was - Archangel Gabriel, then - holding out a dish containing some painted stones she invited me to - "Take one."
Like the hoop drum – one stone called to me – and I picked it up.
"Turn it over" said Joy.
Turning the stone in my hand I saw - painted on its surface - a picture of a wizard, underneath was written the word - Magic.

The stone – I was told – was painted by the Native American lady I had met in the car park in Oak Creek Canyon.

Magic - was indeed the perfect word to sum up the experiences I had, not just today – but throughout this entire visit. Everything that I had seen and experienced could be summed up in the word - Magic.

Beaming from ear to ear – I thanked Joy and Sandra once more – and retired to my room.

Later that evening we all went out to a local Mexican restaurant for dinner. The meal and the service were excellent, as had been the common theme throughout my stay. The waiters appearing from nowhere to refill depleted water glasses – and when thanked – replied with the words – "You're welcome."

It was about 9pm when we left the restaurant and Joy, who was driving asked – "Is there anything else you want to buy?"
I had bought presents for John, the family, friends and myself, but I had not yet found anything for Joy and Sandra. I also wanted to buy a colourful rug on which I could sit whilst playing my drum.

I told Joy about the rug.
"I know where we can get that" she replied.
A couple of minutes later I was inside a shop that sold gifts amongst which - were a selection of colourful rugs. Thankfully, they stayed open 'till 9.30pm.
Browsing around, I found just the rug that I had envisaged and I also found a gift each, for Joy and Sandra.

When we returned home, and before I went to my room - as was the nightly routine – Joy asked: "Are you ready to go home?"

"No - not yet" I truthfully replied – "I've had such a great time, I don't want it to end, and I feel as though I have to do something else – but I don't know what it is." As Joy picked up her drink and made her way to her room, she said, "Sleep well – I'll see you in the morning. Goodnight."

I went to my room and put my music on.

Sitting on the edge of the bed, I looked at all the packages that I had bought, and had yet to pack. Looking at my hoop drum I picked it up and vainly tried to ease it into my rucksack – it wouldn't fit. Determined to carry it as hand luggage on the flight – I decided that I would have to buy another bag tomorrow. So – I deduced – there was no point in packing tonight – I may as well leave it?

Happy with my decision, I lay on the bed and listened to my music.

I "raised my vibrations" and although I didn't go to my familiar "place" where I had met with Silver Cloud, I did see The Angel Gabriel. We had a brief conversation, in which I asked

"Who will be my doorkeeper now?"

"*I will*" he replied.

That night, as I lay down in my bed – it was Gabriel I asked to protect me – and as his energy enfolded me – I fell into restful sleep.

Wednesday 3rd June. Sandra's Birthday.

My last full day in Sedona dawned as bright as all the other days had done.
One of the first things that I did every morning was to stand on the patio and marvel at the huge red rocks dressed in their sunny glow, and reaching upwards towards that - bluest of blue sky's.

After my daily phone call with John, and a call to American Airlines to confirm my flight home, I asked Joy if we could go out so that I could buy another bag. She was only too glad to take me and once more, we drove round those now – familiar roads.

"Before we go to the shop – let's go to Airport Road again" she suggested.
I was only too willing to go again and was looking forward to seeing the view of Sedona in the morning light, as it was now only 8am.
After Joy parked the car and we stepped out into the heat, Joy said, "You wander around – and I'll go and sit and look at the view."

Momentarily, forgetting that Wolf and Silver Cloud were not there, I asked, "Which way shall I go?" Remembering that neither Wolf nor Silver Cloud would answer me, I felt sad and walked on.
I was drawn to walk down a pathway where I found a nice sunny rock to sit on. The views from this position were spectacular.
Sitting there on my rock – I became aware of the presence of the energy that had helped me to ground myself. The energy moved closer to me and my hands and feet began to buzz and tingle.

"Who are you?" I asked.

The reply was:
"I am energy. You will never see me as man - or woman – for I am both.
You will always see me as energy.
My name is Golden Eye."

I was really excited to have had this communication, and by now – the whole of my body was buzzing.
At his suggestion, I placed two sticks that I found nearby, on the ground by me feet – placing them in the form of a cross.
I understood that placing the two sticks together in this manner was a symbol of our commitment to one another.

When Golden Eye and I had finished this brief ceremony – I set off to find Joy and to tell her what had happened.
After I finished my tale – she turned to me and asked:
"Do you think you will ever come back here?"

I considered the question for a second and then asked Golden Eye the same question.
Hearing his answer – I replied – "One day – yes – I will be back, but I am ready to go home now."

Joy and I spent another 15 minutes or so, looking out over the rooftops of Sedona.
Always – my gaze drifting to the mountainous red rocks silhouetted against the blue sky. As we sat side by side, Joy and I began to point out to each other - the many different "faces" that are etched into the rock face.

Faces – not drawn by man – but etched with the eons of time. Faces that tell stories of bravery and hardship, of battles fought and lost. Faces that watch the world in gentle, silent, dignity. Faces that display a "Knowing" and an "Understanding." Faces that are kind.
Faces like those of Silver Cloud, Buffalo, Wolf and White Cloud.

All of whom, I liked to think - were back in their own land - if only for the briefest of visits.

Joy and I left the Airport road and set off to purchase my last minute "must haves" and the all important bag for my hoop drum.
Returning to the shop from which I had bought the first bag – I was greeted by the same lady on the 'till.

She asked me how my visit was going – and where I had been and seemed to be genuinely interested as I recounted some of my visits.
Telling her that this was my last day in Sedona – she wished me a "good journey home" and I said how nice it was to meet her, adding – "I'll call in again when I come back."
We both laughed and I went to rejoin Joy.

As we arrived back at the house - I knew that I had had my last view of Sedona in the daylight – for this trip at least.
I also knew that it was time for me to go home to Wales and to be reunited with John and Jack and Jill.

Declining yet another birthday treat - trip to the cinema – I told Joy and Sandra that I would stay and pack my now expanded - set of luggage.

Having witnessed my many purchases, especially the hoop drum, they laughed at my plight.

Still laughing and wishing me, "Good Luck" they left for the cinema - gently closing the door behind them.

"My Place" at Red Rock Crossing

"My Place" - the "Path to my Right"

Cathedral Rock at Red Rock Crossing

Joy and Sandra at Red Rock Crossing

Another view of Catthedral Rock showing the clear water

Yorrick sunbathing at Red Rock Crossing

Joy (L) myself and Sandra at Red Rock Crossing

Steamboat through the window

Joy, Sandra, Dave & Pat

"Smoke Signal" on the way to the Cave

Me in the mouth of the Cave

Handprints on the walls of the Cave

Sandra, Joy and Pat resting in the Cave

Yorrick sitting in the shade

The "Smoke signal" as seen from the mouth of the Cave

A view taken on our trek down from the Cave

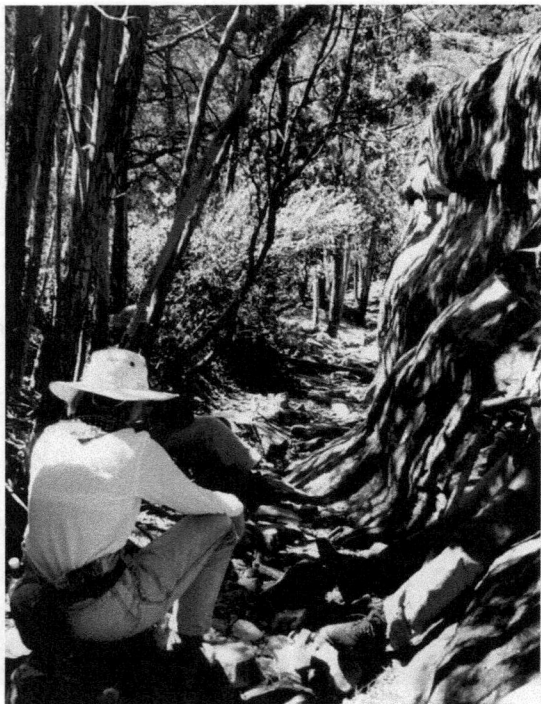

Pat looking down the pathway from the Cave

One more breathtaking view

Yorrick in meditaion on the patio.

An "Angel" drifts by the house.

That is a big Melon!

The Sedona Tram

Yorrick in his window seat on the Tram

Boynton Canyon - showing the caves

Another view of Boynton Canyon

Half a Fire Truck!

Standing on Airport Road - Sedona is far below

Magnificant view across the town of Sedona!

CHAPTER FOUR

SPIRITS IN THE SKY

Thursday 4th June.

It was 5 o'clock in the morning.
My bags were all packed and I was wearing my
favourite "ethnic" purple and green top with the tiny
circular mirrors stitched into it.
My Arizona shoes were waiting for me, by the front
door.

There was just time left for some breakfast – and then a
final check around my room.
(In case you were wondering – my supply of tea bags,
film and cigarettes all ran out and had to be replenished
as and when).
Having checked my room and leaving a Thankyou card
for Joy and Sandra to find later - I closed the door shut
behind me.
With one final look out of the living room window at
the mountain - which remained empty - I said my
goodbyes.

"Bye Silver Cloud"
"Bye Wolf"
"Bye Patio"
"Bye House"
"Thankyou for everything."

The first leg of the journey home was the short trip to
the Motel in Sedona. From here, the 6am shuttle bus
would take me - Yorrick – and Yorricks new found
friend – back to Phoenix.

Driving to the Motel with Joy and Sandra was a somewhat subdued affair.

Obviously it was early in the morning – but more than that – the finality of this journey had subdued us all.

"How would you sum up your trip?" asked Joy.

"There is only one word to describe it – and that is – Brilliant."

"What do you mean – brilliant?" she asked.

"Everything about this trip has been perfect. The things I have seen and done – the places and the timing of everything. The work we have done together – and the things that you have taught me - about me. It has all been brilliant! – Perfect! It could not have been better in any way."

Sandra then said – "Well, you have taught us as well. One thing you taught us, is that it is good to have someone to stay in the house.

You are the first person to have stayed with us. And we now know that it is OK to have someone live in your space for a while. You have always known when Joy and I wanted "time out" and you went to your room or the patio. It has been - to use your word - brilliant."

I was amazed to hear that they had never had a guest to stay in their home before – which only made their invitation more special than I had originally thought.

The conversation turned to some of the funny moments we had shared, and - laughing – we arrived at the Motel.

In just a few minutes time – I would be leaving Sedona and these two wonderful people.

The wait for the shuttle bus to arrive seemed endless.
Now – I wanted the goodbyes to be over quickly – it all felt so final, sad and awkward.
I wanted to be on my way – and I'm sure Joy and Sandra just wanted to get home – and enjoy their space.

The bus arrived on time.
The same driver who had delivered me to Sedona, got out of his seat and placed my luggage - along with the luggage of a few other travellers waiting at the Motel that morning - into the rear of the bus.

My luggage now consisted of:
My original suitcase packed to bulging point.
A red holdall, which partly contained my hoop drum and rug (which I would carry as hand luggage)
And a green holdall which was stuffed full of clothes and presents.

My bulging rucksack, which I hoped would still class as a "handbag" to the airline staff, was lolling at my feet.
The time had come to say goodbye and we three said a somewhat tearful farewell - with lots of hugs and smiles all round.

Climbing into the shuttle bus I sat down in a window seat and waved to Joy and Sandra. As the bus drove out of the car park, we continued to wave to each other - then they were out of sight - and I left Sedona.

What a wonderful, wonderful visit!!

The drive to Phoenix – now in daylight – revealed the wonderful scenery of desert and cacti and as we neared the suburbs of Phoenix, the four wide lanes of the road on which we were travelling, fascinated me. The early morning rush hour traffic seemed to be escorting us on our way to the airport.

As he was nearing the airport the driver asked us all which airline we were flying with and American Airlines – my flight – was the first stop he informed me. The shuttle bus came to a halt directly outside the doorway that led to my check in desk and as soon as he unloaded my luggage a porter dashed out of the terminal, reloaded my bags onto a trolley and dashed back inside the terminal.

Keeping a tight hold of my rucksack - which contained, amongst other things - a sleeping Yorrick and 16 rolls of precious exposed films – I quickly tipped the driver (as is the custom in America) hastily said goodbye – and trotted into the concourse in the wake of the porter and my luggage.

The check-in desk for Chicago was conveniently - just inside the building - and within 10 minutes, my bulging suitcase and the green holdall had been accepted and checked in without any question and had disappeared down the conveyor belt.

"See you in Manchester" I called – full of confidence. In response to the question, "Have you any hand luggage?" I confidently held the red holdall aloft – taking care to keep my rucksack behind my back and out of sight.

The lady looked at the bag and silently passed my boarding pass over – "Have a nice flight" she said – with little enthusiasm.

With the rucksack on my back and clutching firmly onto the bag with the hoop drum – I stepped back out of the building to have a cigarette.

The sun was getting hot – and the blue sky was dappled with a few fluffy white clouds.

More people were arriving for their flights and as I watched them, I wondered if any of them would be on my flight to Chicago.

Finishing my cigarette – I lit another one.

I knew that when I returned to the confines of the terminal – it would be time to say a final Adieu to Phoenix and Arizona - and I wished to delay that moment for just a little longer.

Re entering the concourse I noticed - for the first time – the many policemen that were patrolling the area.

They were all carrying machine guns.

For the second time only, during my trip – I was aware of the possible threat of gun crime in this (and other) countries, and now – sadly – on the streets of the UK.

As the years have gone on – armed police at airports are the norm – but for me then – the sight of those guns was the catalyst that made me to seek out the safe enclosure of the departure lounge.

Phoenix airport is light, modern and clean.

Feeling thirsty, I made my way into the bar, which was near to my departure gate.

Sitting down at the bar, I ordered an orange juice. Whilst I was waiting for my drink to arrive I noticed that sitting on the bar just a few inches away from me was - an ash tray!

"Smoking was allowed" - the bar man assured me and so I happily settled myself down whilst I waited for the public address system to call me to the gate.

It was while I was sitting here that I saw - what for me - was another icon of Americanism and whatsmore – he was heading in my direction!

A smartly, yet casually dressed, sun tanned man of about 30yrs old, came and sat on the bar stool next to mine.

He was dressed in a black jacket, denim jeans and wore a pristine white shirt, which not only enhanced his tan – but also reflected the whiteness of his perfect teeth!

The shirt – worn open to his stomach – revealed a thick gold chain which was hanging down from his neck and on the end of the chain – was a gold medallion about 2in in diameter.

With his jet black, neatly cut hair, white teeth and shirt and the medallion – he was a picture of American suave.

He struck up a conversation with me – you know the sort of thing – "Where are you from? "Where are you going?" etc. Then he began to tell me of his recent life history. He told me that he had a wonderful, beautiful girlfriend and that they had recently returned home from a wonderful, beautiful skiing trip where they had stayed in a very exclusive hotel etc. etc. etc.

I really enjoyed listening to him. The one way conversation passed the time in a very pleasant manner and I just resisted the temptation to take his photograph for my album!

Responding to the public address system, calling passengers for Chicago to the boarding gate – I scooped up my bags. "Well that's me" I announced to the young man, "it's been lovely to meet you – Bye."

"Have a nice Daaay and a safe trip home" he replied.

I joined a throng a people who were also making their way to the boarding gate.

This being my third boarding of a plane – I felt like a "regular" flyer and having stepped onto the plane – I quickly found my seat.

The flight from Phoenix to Chicago was very full.
Once again – I had asked for a window seat and the American Airlines had obliged.
Carefully, I lifted the bag containing my hoop drum, up towards the overhead locker and was relieved when it slid in – just as Joy and Sandra had assured me that it would.
Successfully squashing my rucksack under my seat - "Oops – sorry Yorrick" - I sat down and fastened my seat belt.

Whilst the other passengers were still boarding I had my face glued to the window, watching fuel tankers and other vehicles moving around outside – not wishing to miss anything of my last sights of Phoenix.
I was so engrossed in the activity – that I barely glanced at the young man who came and sat in the seat next to me.

The take off was as thrilling as my first two had been and as we heaved into the sky, I said a silent farewell to Phoenix, Arizona, Joy and Sandra, Sedona and - Silver Cloud and Wolf.

"We're on our way home Yorrick" I said, and I swear that I heard him shout a little "hooray."

As the plane levelled and settled into its flight path, my mind began to review some of the things I had seen and done over the past few days.

I thought about the red rocks and blue sky – my room back in Sedona – the handprints on the cave wall – Silver Cloud standing on the hill – that large ice cream – and my new found fondness for Coke a Cola.

I tried to recall all the gifts I had bought for people.

The gifts that were carefully packed in my luggage, which - I was certain - was now in the hold of the plane?

And I hoped the large poster showing a map of Sedona and its surrounding area - that Joy and Sandra had given me - would survive intact in my suitcase.

My mind was awash with the sights and sounds of the past nine wonderful days. I smiled to myself as I remembered all the fun and laughter that had interspersed those moving, touching, tranquil and peaceful moments.

Something brought my focus and attention back into my immediate surroundings. Glancing down to my left, I noticed that the man sitting next to me had a pad of paper and a pen in his hand.

He was drawing different symbols all over the page.

The drawings were random – not like shorthand, not merely "doodles" – and he seemed to be engrossed in what he was doing.

I glanced at him and he, noticing me looking – stared at me. In fact he seemed to stare through me - and I found his stare quite unnerving.

I turned my head to look through the window.

"What" I thought, "were the symbols?"

"What did they mean?"
It seemed a very strange thing to be doing.

A few minutes later, I glanced back at the notepad – he had turned the page and was continuing to draw.

Now - whether it was tiredness on my part I don't know – but my unease continued to grow, especially after we exchanged yet another glance – and I saw that his eyes remained – well - almost empty.

Silently I called: "Help – I don't like this man's energy!"

No sooner had the words left my mind, I saw – floating above the heads of the people sat in the seats in front of me - and down the plane towards me – Gabriel in all his etheric finery.
Gabrielle's energy flowed over and around me – and around those people several rows in front and behind me.

Two minutes later – the man put his pad and pen away, and went to sleep.

I thanked Gabriel profusely.

The flight continued on its peaceful track, and I resumed my watch through the window.
We flew high over a landscape that was criss crossed with long straight roads, roads that seemed to go on endlessly.
I saw aerial views of Ranches - the owners of which appeared to have no neighbours.
I watched as the sun beat onto the ground, casting shadows 33,000 ft below.

And I marvelled at the cloudless blue sky.

About an hour later – as the plane neared O'Hare airport, Chicago - I saw some of those tall buildings that had been obscured by the mist 11 days ago.
My fellow passenger on that day had been right – the Chicago skyline is a wonderful view.

Having disembarked at Chicago I found my way to the check in desk for Manchester and duly - checked in. With my boarding pass and passport safely in my bag, I made my way to the exit of the concourse to have a cigarette.

The sun was hot – the sky – not quite as blue and clear as in Phoenix.
I found that, yet again, I was not the only smoker in transit that day. A small group of "addicts" with the same affliction – were huddled together at the corner of the building. I went to join them.
However pathetic - the none smokers amongst you - feel that we smokers are – there is an instant camaraderie within this band of outcasts.
A common "ailment" that brings us together, regardless of title, money, sex or age.
And so, within the comfort of this group of people – I stood watching the familiar succession of white limousines and other vehicles, disgorging their cargo with efficient speed.

Having satisfied my nicotine withdrawal – I returned into the terminal.
I had told John that I would try to ring him at some point on my journey home so I looked around for a telephone.

Spotting a bank of public telephones against a wall – I walked over to a vacant one.

Reaching into my rucksack, I retrieved my little blue notebook.

The notebook that I had filled in every day – and that I have referred to now, in order to write these chapters.

In the back of the notebook I had written down the number of the international operator who dealt with reverse charge calls – or as they say in America – collect calls.

Having got through to the operator and given her our home telephone number, I waited, then I heard the phone ringing. Waiting with bated breath – I heaved a sigh of relief when I heard John's voice on the other end of the line.

"Hello – it's me!" I shouted.

"Hi – how are you, and where are you?" John asked.

"I'm in Chicago!" I announced - with all the finesse of an excitable 5yr old.

After a brief conversation, during which I informed him that my flight was due to leave on time and therefore would land in Manchester at 8.30am tomorrow – Friday – we said goodbye, and hung up our respective telephones.

Picking up the hoop drum bag that I had securely held between my Arizona shoes – I spoke to Yorrick – "Just time for another cigarette Yorrick, and then I'll take you home."

I must tell you:

Whilst waiting to board the flight to Manchester – I had to visit the Ladies.

Why do they make these facilities so small!

Wanting to exit the cubicle – I replaced my bulging rucksack over my right shoulder and picked up the bag containing the hoop drum, in my left hand. Standing sidewards, and using the thumb and first finger of my right hand – I withdrew the lock and pulled the door towards me.

The door wedged into my shoulder, knocking me sidewards against the cubicle wall – and with one fell swoop, there I was – stuck.

Grunting – I tried to jiggle my rucksack but it wouldn't budge – nor could I close the door. My precious hoop drum was groaning under the strain of my tilting body and was in serious danger of ending up in the toilet bowl, with me sat on top of it.

How undignified would that have been!

Just as thought I would have to shout for the Emergency Services – the door freed itself and I was catapulted out into the corridor.

Thankfully – there was no one to witness my dilemma – except, "them upstairs" – who, no doubt thought it was hilarious.

Gaining my composure – I completed my ablutions and swept out of the exit with as much dignity as I could muster.

There were a lot of passengers for flight AA 54 to Manchester that day.

I was standing amidst a throng of other passengers near to the gate, all of us awaiting the welcome announcement to "board."

Through the melee of people, a young man emerged. He came up to me and asked: "Am I at the right gate for the flight to Manchester, England?"

"Yes" I replied – "I'm on that flight – so follow me."
"Thankyou very much" he replied "I get confused at airports."
I smiled sympathetically.

The fact that the young man spoke in broken English – and was Chinese - did not curb the elation that I felt at that moment.
I said to myself:
"He must have thought that I looked as though I was a frequent flyer! Used to travelling by plane."
My confidence grew in stature!
I had achieved that goal of 11 days ago – to be a confident, frequent, flyer!!
"I" - I said to myself - "Am a citizen of the world!"
 And it felt - Brilliant!

I happily boarded the aeroplane and located my seat. Undaunted and unhurried by the push of the queue behind me, I carefully placed my hoop drum into the overhead compartment. It was a bit of a tight squeeze as the bubble wrap that I had wrapped the drum in, added to the bulk. But I managed it and breathing a sigh of relief, I sat down.

My seat was located about halfway down the body of the plane, and yet again, I had been given a window seat. As I settled myself and Yorrick into our space – I watched for the young man that I had spoken to earlier.
He came walking up the aisle and smiled and nodded as he went past me.
Still - the passengers kept coming and I began to wonder if the airline had over booked the seats!
My attention kept returning to that overhead locker, especially when I heard the sound of the passengers

around me pushing their bags and briefcases into the same space.

"Please - protect my drum" I implored Gabriel and Golden Eye.

Most people had found their seats – but there was a man and woman standing in the aisle a couple of rows behind me - having a discussion with a member of the cabin crew.

Suddenly the member of cabin crew leant over the woman sitting next to me and said, "Would you mind changing seats?"

She explained that a family of four – mum, dad and two children, had been unable to book seats together.
This meant that one of the children would have to sit a few rows away from its parent.

The crew-member then indicated to me, a vacant seat on the opposite side of the plane, and much nearer the front of the aircraft.

Happy to oblige – I stood up and prepared to remove my hoop drum out of the overhead locker.
"You can leave your bag there if you wish", the crew member informed me.
Leave my drum! Never!
Just as the mother wanted her child close to her - there was no way that I was moving seats and leaving my hoop drum all on its own!

"No" I replied, "If you don't mind – I will take it with me."

Peering into the locker, I realised that I would have to remove a briefcase and a small holdall in order to release my drum.

I removed the holdall and - wearing my best smile I spoke to the watching faces. "Sorry about this", I announced – "I'll just be a minute."
Looking down at the lady who I had been sitting next to, I asked: "Could you just hold this for a minute please?"
"Certainly" she replied – holding out her arms.
Grinning – she held the holdall - which freed my hands, so that I could remove the briefcase.

"I'll hold that" came a male voice from across the aisle.
"Oh – thankyou very much", I said – turning to hand the case to him.
I reached into the locker and gently squeezed my drum out of the locker.
Placing the drum on the floor – I carefully replaced the holdall and the briefcase and closed the locker door.

With the gratitude and obvious relief of the parents ringing in my ears and - looking over the heads of my fellow passengers - I focused my eyes on my new destination – it seemed to be a long way away.

Now I am not a large person – but the journey down the aisle was a slow one. Made more cumbersome because – in my right hand, and leading the way – was Yorrick within the confines of the rucksack – and following on behind, in my left hand – I held the red holdall, which held my hoop drum.

I squeezed my way down the narrow aisle - repeatedly saying, "Excuse me – excuse me – oops – sorry –

excuse me" - as myself, or one of my bags, brushed past someone's coiffured hairdo.

I was reminded once more, of the comedy film "Airplane", especially the scene in which the air stewardess walks down the aisle carrying a guitar. As she passes by the seated passengers, the guitar hits them on the side of the head – and you hear the boing, boing, boing noise of an acoustic guitar reverberating as it hits something solid.
By the time I reached my seat – (thankfully, a window seat) – I must have "introduced" myself to half of the passengers.

Arriving at the vacant seat - and placing my bags on the floor - I spoke to the man sitting in the seat alongside.

"Hello – I'm coming to sit next to you?"
"Hello" he quietly replied.
He didn't look too enthralled with the idea – "Maybe he was tired?" I surmised.

Reaching for the closed locker door – I pulled it open.
I found, to my dismay, that it was full of blue blankets.

Realising that there were many pairs of eyes watching my every move – and feeling happy and confident with a hint of "devilment" - I decided to have some fun!

"Right" I announced to the audience. "I need to put my drum in this locker and it is full of blankets - who would like a blanket? It can get very cold during the night – you'll be grateful for a blanket at 3 o'clock in the morning."

It's amazing isn't it – that once one person wants something – other people want "it" as well.

Two rows behind me – one man put his hand in the air. Laughing, he shouted - "I'll take one."
I passed a blanket to the man in the seat behind and he passed it behind him.
Other passengers put their hands in the air to receive a blanket and a few passengers even stood up to direct the blankets to the waiting hands.
As the blankets travelled along - carried over the heads of the people – their movement resembled a blue "Mexican Wave."

This simple "game" was enjoyed by the playful adults - and an air of bon ami filled the plane.
People were laughing and talking to their neighbours.

When the locker was empty – I thanked the passengers for their help and carefully placed my drum in its copious space.
The man who had remained seated next to the empty seat – stood to let me pass. Tucking my rucksack under my seat – I sat down and fastened my seat belt.
I had exhausted myself!

The plane took off and soared into the sky. As the plane climbed and the ground moved further and further away, I looked through the window and said:
"Thankyou America – see you again sometime."

It was then that I realised that many of the passengers – including the man in the next seat – had spoken with an English accent.
Like me - they too - were returning home.

I wondered if they had stayed in Chicago – or had travelled on to another destination.

I wondered what they had seen and done.

I felt – that out of all of them – I MUST have had the best time.

About 20 minutes into the flight, the female cabin crew who had asked me to change seats, stopped in the aisle by my seat. Leaning across the man sitting next to me she said, "American Airlines would like to thank you for changing your seat – and we would like you to accept this as a gift."

The "this" was a bottle of champagne.

"Thankyou very much!" I exclaimed – and took the bottle off her.

Turning to the now, smiling man in the next seat I asked, "Do you drink champagne?"

Laughing – he said, "I'll drink anything."

"I'd like you to have this then" - handing the bottle to him.

"Are you serious?" he asked.

"Yes, of course" I replied – "I hope you enjoy it."

"Thanks very much indeed" he exclaimed.

He then got out of his seat, walked towards the rear of the plane, taking the bottle with him.

A few minutes later he returned to his seat with a plastic cup, which - I presumed - contained champagne.

"I've shared the champagne with my friends who are sitting further down the plane" he explained.

Just then there were shouts of "Yoo Hoo! – thankyou –
Yoo Hoo!"

I undid my safety belt, stood up and turned round.

Standing, in various parts of the aeroplane, were about
eight men and woman – all raising their plastic cups
and saying "Cheers!"

Other passengers were turning round, laughing and
joining in the fun.

I accepted their thanks and with a huge grin across my
face – I sat back in my seat.

Sipping from his plastic cup – the man began to talk to
me. He explained that he and his companions were
work colleagues and that they were returning from a
week long Business Convention, which had been held
in San Diego.

San Diego – he said – was a wonderful city, a city that
he intended to return to at some time in the future – but
as a tourist.

He than asked me where I had been and I told him a
little about the red rocks, the desert and the dog that
wore a sun visor.

This Manchester flight was a nightime flight and as the
sun began to sink on the horizon, I took every
opportunity to stare out of the window, taking in the
last views of the vast land below, criss crossed with
those straight roads that ran North to South and East to
West, and as the plane flew over the sea, I averted my
eyes upward to gaze at the passing clouds.

Unable to sleep, I continued to watch the sky and at
some point, just before dawn, I noticed that another
aeroplane was travelling practically parallel with us.

Sitting upright in my seat I fixed my gaze on the other plane. "Was it just a trick of the light – or was that plane drifting towards us?"

I wondered if the pilot of our plane had seen it, and momentarily thought that maybe I should mention it to a member of the cabin crew.

"Golden Eye – What is that plane doing?" I asked.

No sooner had I asked the question, and, as if in answer to it – the other plane seemed to alter its course away from us.

As the other plane moved away – I wondered if a passenger on it was also awake and had looked out of the window and seen us.

I wondered where its destination was, and I wondered at the wonder of the Universe.

The Universe that had brought these two planes containing many souls - together over the Atlantic – just as dawn was breaking on the 5th May 1998.

I felt so grateful and fortunate to have been given the opportunity to experience this entire trip.

Grateful to Joy and Sandra for inviting me.

Grateful to John who did all that he could to make this trip happen.

And grateful to Silver Cloud who had given me the tools I needed to find the courage to step on the plane.

I had had many, many personal - magical moments during this trip: –

Sitting under the pine tree with Silver Cloud and Wolf.

My time spent at Red Rock Crossing.

My time spent with Joy and Sandra.

The trip to Flagstaff and the snow - the dog wearing his sun visor.

My visit to the Church of the Holy Cross.

And the visit to that wonderful circus.

But by and large – these magical moments were so personal that they couldn't be shared and felt by others. And I was bursting with gratitude.

Those moments on the aeroplane – culminating in the gift of the Champagne – could be shared with others.

The magic of the spirit at play - can be consumed and utilised by others.

I felt humbled and glad.
Humble - to have been the recipient of all the magical moments.
And Glad - that after all those good things I had received from Spirit - Joy and Sandra - and everyone that I had met along the journey – I was able to share - albeit briefly - some of the joy that I was feeling - amongst those – Spirits in the sky.

Looking out of the window as we flew over England – I looked onto a scene of grey clouds.
Yes – it was still raining.
However, the sight of the green fields below – was a very welcome sight indeed.
Having placed my watch back on GMT and listening to the captains' voice over the loud-speaker system – I realised that we would be landing in 20 minutes.

In a short time – I would see John again! I had so much to tell him, so much had happened during my trip.

I had seen and experienced so many things and my head was buzzing with it all. So much had changed in 11 hectic days – 11 days that felt both - like a lifetime, and merely, just a few hours.

Although we had spoken every morning – I wondered how he was? You never really know until you see them do you? And I wondered how Jack and Jill were, and would they be as pleased to see me, as I would be to see them? I wondered if John had managed to dodge the showers and cut the grass and I wondered if Joy and Sandra were sitting on the patio, watching the white fluffy clouds float by.

Silver Cloud and Wolf were not with me – and I was sad about that – and I wondered if someone had told them that I was nearly home?

And my thoughts turned to Angel Gabriel and Golden Eye – and I wondered if they would like my music – wondered what changes would take place when I began to work with them.

My mind flitted between Sedona and the future and just when I thought that my wonderings were making me dizzy – I realised that I was feeling a little dizzy.

The plane was banking round in a big circle. The view out of my window was of fields, building and roads – all, at what felt like, a very acute angle!

Round we went again, and just as I was beginning to feel a little "stressed" – the plane began to level off.

The captains' voice came over the tannoy.

"Sorry about that, ladies and gentlemen, we had to wait for our slot. I am pleased to tell you that we are now free to land. The temperature is (I can't remember) and there is a light drizzle."

"Thankyou for flying American Airlines."

Standing in the baggage hall, I was pleased to see that my suitcase and holdall were one of the first bags on the conveyor belt. Hauling it onto a trolley, and carefully placing the hoop drum on the top, I confidently followed the signs and arrows to the exit.
This time – the walk through the customs desk was a very quick affair – a quick flash of my passport – and I was done. A few paces further on, another customs officer stepped in front of me, causing me to halt.
"Where have you flown from?" he asked.
"Chicago" I announced proudly.
"Thankyou", he replied, stepping aside to let me pass.

Grateful that he wasn't going to search through my dirty washing – I walked out through the exit.

A smiling John was waiting directly opposite the exit – and - I gratefully noticed – he was holding one of my coats over his arm.
We sat and talked for a few minutes, and I had a cigarette. It felt weird, being back in England.
Although I had been travelling for around 23 hrs, with no sleep – I felt as though, in a matter of seconds, I had just stepped straight out of one world and into another.

The grey skies and the accompanying drizzle remained with us all the way home. But as we were driving along, I realised just how much I had missed the green fields and trees. And spying a sheep in a field – I could not stop myself shouting – "Oh look – there's a sheep."

Once home and reunited with and excitable Jack and Jill – John and I sat down.
I talked, whilst he listened.

Then, in order to give him the gifts I had bought for him, I got my bags into the living room and proceeded to empty their contents all over the living room floor.

It was just after that, when the tiredness hit me and I had to go to bed.

In fact I slept for hours.

Over the next few days – the "jet lag" really kicked in and I slept and slept.

Forecourt of the Motel in Sedona

Outside Phoenix Airport

John with his Winnie the Pooh windsock "pressie"

Me back home, with my lovely spinning windsock.

CHAPTER FIVE

GOLDEN EYE

True to his word – I never saw Golden Eye as a person.
Always – he was a golden light.

A light that shimmered and constantly moved around
and inside me.

His presence - culminating in the buzzing of my hands
– as they are buzzing now as he has come to help me
write this chapter.

Golden Eye took advantage of the confidence that I was
feeling when I returned from America – and his
constant, underlying message was:

"You can be anything you want to be"

At those times when I was feeling "challenged" – either
by circumstance or person – he would whisper in my
ear:

"Shine – and Be Nice"

Seeing and hearing those words again brings a smile to
my face. His words, and my action, have eased my path
on many an occasion.

Golden Eye compared the physical ages of man - to that
of the changing seasons.

On the 21st November 1998 he gave me the following
piece:

HARVEST.

SPRING.

"The World and your spirit have come
to an agreement.
You are to be born on a certain day –
in a certain place – to certain parents.
The earth has been prepared.
Things have been made ready for your arrival.
You have been waiting to return to this new life.
The dawn of a new age begins."

SUMMER.

"Long days – to experience as much of
the new world as you can.
So much has changed, and yet remains the same.
Have you done this before?
Visited this place before?
What - if anything has changed from the last time?
Do you want to change anything?"

AUTUMN.

"In this present life – now is the time to change
what does not harmonise with you.
A time to reflect on the changes.
A time to reflect on the similarities.
As nature around you, begins her preparation for the
coming spring – so you too begin your preparation for
your return home.
But first, you make those changes.
Prepare to leave the soil in a rich, balanced condition –
awaiting the arrival of the next seed."

WINTER.

"A time to reflect and bring together
the lessons of the past year.
A time to come together with those around you.
To reach out to those who need your help and comfort.
For winter can be long or short – time is fickle."

HARVEST.

"A time to enjoy the benefits of what you have sown.
A time to wither – if you have neglected your crop.
A good harvest – and you will return home
ready and willing for a rest.
If your harvest failed this time – then you will have
learned a valuable lesson and your need for
nourishment at your next spring – will feed not just
yourself – but many others."

On the 11th of September 2001 – or as the Americans now simply refer to – "9/11" – Golden Eye and myself were flying back from Mallorca.

At the kind invitation of a friend who lives on the island, I had spent a very enjoyable few days holiday.

But on the 11th of September – I was flying back to Manchester, the take off from Palma airport was to be a "first" for me.

Before we taxied down the runway, the captain warned of expected turbulence. Apparently, the wind was blowing off the hills that surrounded Palma airport and was travelling across our runway.

"The turbulence shouldn't last for too long" – he reassured us, adding – "But we will be climbing through it."

Not knowing quite what to expect – I braced myself. The lady, who was sitting next to me, and I - exchanged weak smiles.

As the plane lifted into the air, everything seemed normal. Suddenly the plane lurched and began to bounce up and down.

As it continued to bounce – first one way, and then another – and against a backdrop of "Oohs" and "Aghaas" from some of the other passengers - I repeated the words that Golden Eye had given me:-

"Shine and be nice" – "Shine and be nice"

And then:

"Golden Eye – it's not working!"

Needless to say – the pilot flew the plane safely through the turbulence and as the plane levelled off onto its flight path, we continued, unhindered, towards Manchester. We were due to land at 3pm.

About 40 minutes out of Manchester, and with the turbulence a distant memory – I began to feel agitated – confined in my seat – and found myself looking at my watch every few minutes.

I didn't understand my agitation – I just knew that I didn't want to be in the air any longer - I just wanted to get off!

The plane landed on schedule and I and my fellow passengers disembarked.

Standing amongst the usual melee of a busy baggage hall, I heard the young lady who was standing nearest to me, speaking on her mobile phone. "What" she exclaimed down the phone – "In America!"

Why? - I wondered, irritably – as she nudged in front of me to retrieve her luggage - do young people always have to have their phone stuck to their ear?

Spotting my bag, I picked it up and went through the exit to meet John who had driven to the airport to meet me, and we chatted all the way home.

We hadn't been home long, before the telephone rang. It was our friend Sue, on the other end of the line. She sounded upset and suggested that we put the television on, as something "awful" had happened in America.

Shocked – and in total dismay – John and I watched the un-folding story.

Watched with horror - as the fate of the passengers and crew who had been on those planes, and those who had been in and around the "Twin Towers" in New York - slowly emerged.

I realised that at the same time as my plane was landing in Manchester – a plane had hit one of the towers.
Now I understood my agitation during my flight.
I understood that the fear and horror that those souls on those planes had emitted - had reverberated throughout the Universe.
I understood that I had felt that reverberation.

I remembered, when I was returning from Chicago how I had seen that other plane travelling alongside.
And I remember how I marvelled at the wonders of the Universe.
That wondrous Universe which brings souls together for one fleeting moment in time.

"There but for the Grace of God - go I"

Before I had left for Mallorca I had heard a new piece of music that I had instantly fallen in love with.
John and I had a "New World" compilation tape – which contained fragments of new music that The New World Music Company was launching.
As so often happens in my life – I knew that I needed to work with this piece of music – I knew that it would facilitate another forward step in my life.
"This music – to me – is a Benediction"
I announced to John.

On the 2nd of November 2001 I was thrilled when the postman delivered a package containing a new CD that John had ordered for me via the Internet.
The title of the CD is "Tranquility" and it is written and composed by David Sun.

That same day – John was flying to Mallorca, not on a holiday – but a working trip.

With just myself and Jack and Jill to consider – I relished the opportunity to sit and work with the music.

I walked the dogs in the early afternoon and then shut myself in my workroom with my music.

As soon as I "sat" – I was transported to what can only be described as a roof–less Cathedral.
From my vantagepoint at the back of the Cathedral – I could see that I was alone.

The pews that were laid out before me glowed in a golden light. I sat down on a nearby step and waited.
As I waited – the light, the pews, and all the other fixtures and fittings of such a grand building – gradually disappeared and I was now sitting in the ruins of a cathedral.

In an instant – I knew that Golden Eye was leaving.
In that same instant – I felt his energy leave my body.
With my head bent towards the floor, and through my instantaneous tears – I saw a pair of sandled feet.

My new Guide had come.

I wasn't ready to speak to a new Guide! The pain that I was feeling was immense. Without lifting my head and unable to speak any words – I left the Cathedral, and left my room - seeking the solace of the living room.

Later – I wrote in my notebook:

"The energy who has given me so much is no longer within me.
He taught me to be me.

Taught me to say what I wanted – to say what I didn't – and to know the difference."

"He helped me to be more understanding of people –
but also to speak my Truth.

He made me understand that there is an easy way to
live – and a difficult way – the choice is mine.

He has helped many people while we have been
together – sometimes over a period of time –
sometimes in a sentence.

His distant healing has great strength and has changed
lives – often overnight.

Many Spirits have returned Home, with his help.

I know that I must celebrate when a Guide moves on.
I will – tomorrow.

For now – I must return to my room. To remember and
thank Golden Eye for all that he has done."

Returning to my room, my writing continued as I spoke
to him:

"I am picking up the stones that we collected in
Sedona.

I am sorry for all those times I forgot to thank you.
I am sorry for those times when I 'lost it' and for falling
asleep three nights ago without saying 'Goodnight.'

As I am sitting, I find myself in 'our' cave and my new
Guide comes for me.
Together we stand and watch the distant sunset, and
feel the warmth."

"The sky is awash with a pinky orange colour, which moves and sinks slowly to our right.

Goodnight Golden Eye.

I will see you in every sunset."

I sat up into the early hours of the next day – still listening to "Tranquilty."

The "Benediction" had taken place hours ago – yet still I cried – and the emptiness that I felt gnawed away at me.

"Who is going to tell me to...?"

"Shine?" - answered the man who had jumped down from the Cross.

I will end this chapter with a verse that was channelled through me on the 21st November 1998.
The name of the speaker is not known.

"Weep not for those who have died.
For death is only in the minds of the living.

Think not that they have gone forever
But that their life continues in a beautiful place.

A place that is filled with anything the heart desires.
A place where love is all consuming.
Where joy is found in the realisation of one's
own existence.

Weep not for those who have died.
For they smile down on you – for ever."

Channelled on the 21st November 1998. Annon.

THE JOURNEY

Dear Reader,

Those of you who know me will no doubt be expecting some witty retort – by way of ending this book - and therefore the trilogy. But now that I have finished writing – I am at a loss as to what to say…

When I began to write about my journey into Mediumship – I thought that I would be writing one book.
The title – "More Friends Than You Know" – was given to me on the 19th June 1994 - by my first "working" Guide – William.
The prospect was pretty daunting and readers will know that I was reminded - by Spirit - several times over a period of years - to begin my task!
Nearing the end of writing "More Friends", and feeling both relieved and excited – Silver Cloud, White Cloud, Buffalo and Wolf visited me.

"We want to be in the same book", they said.

They told me to continue telling my story under the title of, "Spirits In The Sky."
The sight of the great pile of notebooks to be re-opened was a challenge. But as the weeks went on – and encouraged as I was by the generous response of readers to the first book – I really enjoyed writing it.

Nearing the end of writing that book – I realised that the completed story was just too long for one volume.
Asking the advice of my "Team" - I was given the third title - "Spirits Fly High."

Well – I have loved sharing those memories with you and as I arrive at the end of that particular story and therefore - the trilogy - I have now completed the task set before me by my Native American Spirit Team.

The journey that I have been on whilst writing the trilogy - has personally - been tremendous.

It has been:

A journey of happy and sad memories.

A journey of re-visiting - and remembering communications.

A journey that has given me an opportunity to hear - once more - forgotten lessons from the past.

It has been a journey that has allowed me to be close to all those visitors – especially Silver Cloud, White Cloud, Buffalo and Wolf.

They taught me the skills that I needed to be a medium. They guided and protected me through some tough times. They walked with me over a period of years and were my constant companions.

Their teachings, guidance, humour and unconditional love – not just for myself – but for others – remains a humbling experience.
Words cannot express my gratitude to them all.

I am privileged to have worked with the American Indian.
I am very, very fortunate to have worked with Silver Cloud, White Cloud, Buffalo and Wolf.

I hope that one of them will return soon so that I can tell them, face to face, that I wrote - *"As is."*

As my current guide – Joseph, my doorkeeper - Hanna and I continue to move forward on our journey - our hope is that individually – each book tells its own story.

Collectively – they cover some 46yrs of my life, which is more than half of my life expectancy I should think! But far, far more important than that:

Collectively – they tell a story of the unconditional love and guidance that the Spirit World wishes to give to us.
A Spirit World which is far away – and yet so near to our everyday life.
A Spirit World which teaches us not to judge others.
A Spirit World which heals – and teaches us to heal.
A collective Spirit which cares for our well being and very existence – even when we cannot care ourselves.

A collective Spirit, with whom we will all rejoin - in the not too distant future.

The trilogy tells us that each and every one of us has "Friends" – "Spirits" and the ability to "Fly."

Good luck on your own journey.

Thankyou for "listening."
Bye for now.
Love Lynn

Spirits Fly High

ADIEU

"Dear Reader

Our aim, when commissioning this book, was to share the story – the journey travelled – by one woman who was willing to devote her time and energy, to learning and experiencing the power, love and understanding – that is, The Spirit World.

Her mission – to share those experiences with others through the written word.

A mission that she was reluctant to fulfil – but a mission, that she is glad – is now concluded.

As a group – representing the Indian race and heritage – our work with the channel is completed.

The team, are no more and yet, will remain forever.

We wish you well.
We wish you joy.
We wish you adieu."

Silver Cloud

White Cloud

Buffalo

Wolf

Channelled by Lynn Quigley on 29th April 2007

More Friends Than You Know
(Book One of the Trilogy)

I recognise now, that all through my life, profound and poignant happenings and meetings have usually been marked with the receiving of an object, a keep-sake, the energy of the happening or meeting being held within it, in the same way as a precious crystal holds within it's form, energy, knowledge and it's own unique healing power.

(extract from Chapter Two)

Lying in bed that same night, I was suddenly aware that a man in a dark suit was standing very close to my side of the bed – just standing staring at me – saying nothing.
I dived under the bed covers and said the only thing that I knew to say – "Go to the light – Go to the light". I lay and listened. Hearing nothing – I peeped out from under the covers to see if he had gone.
No – he was still there.

(extract from Chapter Eight)

ISBN 978-0-9534946-3-7

Spirits In The Sky

(Book Two of the Trilogy)

"Death itself is a return Home – but as we grow – our Home changes – the distance changes – we have to keep going further, further Home.

We do not know where our next Home will be. The passage of time takes us to our next Home."

Kato

(extract from Chapter Four)

"Those of us outside your Universe, wish you to know that we are there to help and assist, and that the visual aids that we have – show us that the planet Earth is indeed, in need of help and assistance. This is why wecome – to aid the planet Earth, so that it can continue its' path within it's own solar system, which, in turn, aids the path of other planets in similar solar systems."

Peter

(extract from Chapter Eleven)

ISBN 978-0-9534946-4-4

Up to date information about Lynn, her
other publications and contact details can
be found on her website:

www.GoldenCloud.co.uk

www.ingramcontent.com/pod-product-compliance
Lightning Source LLC
Chambersburg PA
CBHW062215080426
42734CB00010B/1905